LEARN TO LUCID DREAM

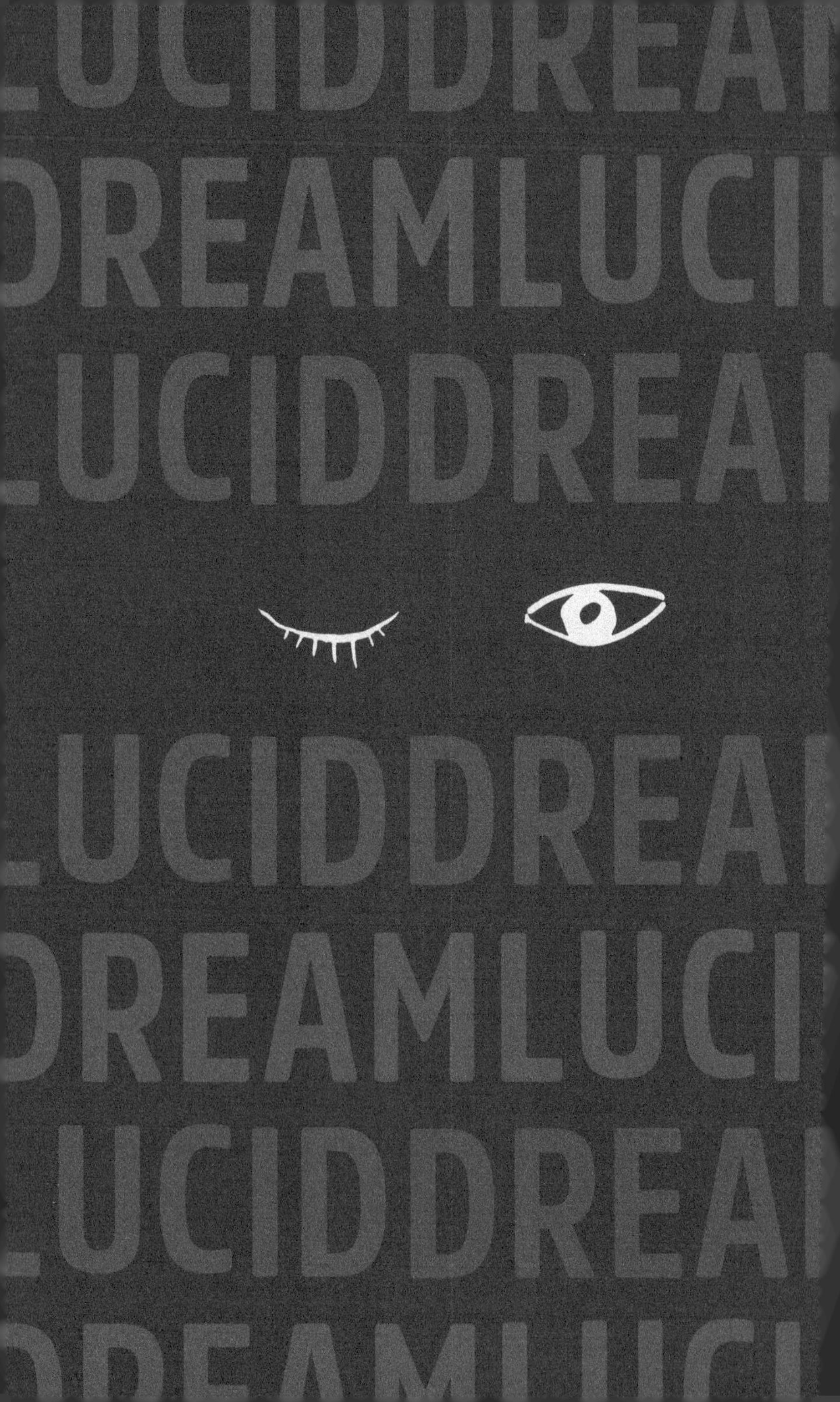

LEARN TO
LUCID
DREAM

POWERFUL TECHNIQUES FOR AWAKENING
CREATIVITY AND CONSCIOUSNESS

KRISTEN LaMARCA, PhD

ROCKRIDGE
PRESS

With unconditional love, this book is dedicated to my teachers and loved ones, particularly my parents, who have had a profound impact on me.

Interior and Cover Designer: Emma Hall
Art Producer: Sue Bischofberger
Editor: David Lytle
Production Editor: Ashley Polikoff

ISBN: Print 978-1-64152-382-0 | eBook 978-1-64152-383-7

CONTENTS

INTRODUCTION

ALL HUMAN BEINGS POSSESS A PRICELESS GIFT—the ability to explore a state that offers intuitive wisdom and guidance for understanding consciousness, who we are, and where we are headed.

We enter this state every night when we fall asleep and begin to dream. Few people in the modern world hold a deep, genuine appreciation of dreams, let alone the skills to apply their dreams toward nourishing their waking lives. Even fewer people realize their potential to radically alter their dream experience to benefit themselves and others—known as the extraordinary art of *lucid dreaming*.

In ordinary dreams, you don't think about your state of consciousness. You assume that you're awake, which limits your range of possible experiences.

To become lucid in a dream, then, means that you're directly reflecting on your state of being and realize: "Aha! Here I am, dreaming." This clear recognition of the dream's true nature crosses a threshold from your usual mode of dreaming. You now have a new "frame" on your reality, granting you freer access to experiences.

This book's goal is to introduce you to lucid dreaming, and to teach you not only how to do it, but also how to begin applying it toward improving your life.

If you've been interested in lucid dreaming, you're probably aware that there's no lack of resources available about how to dream lucidly—a lot of comprehensive, in-depth work has already been done in this area by previous generations.

However, there hasn't been a short, updated guide that digests the best available information, and organizes it in step-by-step tools that are easy to understand, remember, and apply. The goal is to offer you these tools with more precision and simplicity than is currently available for beginners.

This book was motivated by my interest in applying lucid dreaming toward studying consciousness and treating mental health disorders. My personal journey into lucid dreaming was sparked during my early studies in psychology, when I learned that lucid dreaming is scientifically verifiable, and that with training, it can also be a nightly occurrence. I was fascinated by the expansive spectrum of possibilities for how this state could benefit me and others, which motivated me to learn to lucid dream myself.

My early development as a lucid dreamer was interwoven with my training as a clinical psychologist and researcher. In 2007, I attended my first intensive retreat with Stephen LaBerge, the prominent lucid dreaming expert, and soon I began researching and teaching with him. Later, we authored a study showing that combining the over-the-counter memory enhancer galantamine (see page 62) with the skills for inducing lucidity substantially increases the odds of lucid dreaming compared to a placebo.

During graduate school, I integrated my growing knowledge about lucid dreaming into my training in treating psychological conditions. In providing lucid dreaming therapy, I saw firsthand that lucid dreaming can let patients see and think without their usual defenses.

Through the lens of lucidity, they can face their fears more creatively, process emotions better, and get to know themselves in ways that can be gentle and playful, easing them along a path toward healing.

My own lucid dreaming experiences have been nothing short of transformative. Some of my lucid dreams have completely altered my views of myself and how I understand reality. They have added much meaning to my life, which over time keeps growing and weaving itself in with new dreams and waking experiences.

My lucid dreams also help me in small but important day-to-day ways. No matter life's ups or downs, or what circumstances I'm trying to negotiate, my lucid dreams have always acted as a mirror that I could hold up to help me see what, within myself, I need to look at most.

I've also appreciated what I might call lucid dreaming's "secondary benefits," which taught me how to better focus my mind and attention, set and follow through on intentions, prioritize my higher values, and be more observant in my waking life.

Since you are reading this, you too must be curious about lucid dreaming's profound potential. Which is why I've packed this book with the most essential tools for becoming a true *oneironaut*—someone trained to optimally explore the dream state.

With the right motivation and techniques, learning how to dream lucidly is easier than you might think. If you're just starting out, some of the ideas in this book might seem different or strange, while others might feel highly intuitive. Take your time learning the practices offered. That way, you can best integrate them with your daily routines, and allow your dreams the space they need to expand into one of your greatest creative resources. Learning lucid dreaming will shine a light on many new pathways toward self-discovery, so stay open and curious, and enjoy the ride.

CHAPTER 1

A BRIEF OVERVIEW OF LUCID DREAMING

Lucid dreaming grants you access to modes of consciousness that offer personal, spiritual, and creative benefits. The ability to lucid dream is not as rare as you'd think. Most people recall at least one lucid dream, and about a quarter of the population dreams lucidly at least once a month. But through proper training, you can substantially improve the frequency and quality of your lucid dreams. By learning how to optimize the mind-set and physical conditions that are conducive to lucidity, the world of lucid dreaming becomes much more accessible.

To begin, let's review the definitions and benefits of lucid dreaming. How can you expect your lucid dreaming skills to grow as you embark on this journey? The truth is that your experience will vary depending on your individual context, but I'll touch on the general trajectory for moving from being a beginner to an expert. I'll also trace the Western history of lucid dreaming, summarizing the most influential researchers' pioneering works. I'll also touch on the prominent theories about what dreams mean and what they're for.

What Is Lucid Dreaming?

In his 1913 work *A Study of Dreams*, Frederik van Eeden defined lucid dreaming as an awareness within dreams. He explained that in lucid dreams, you know that you are dreaming, can remember the conditions of your daily life and sleeping body, and can direct your attention toward your highest values.

Van Eeden also explained that you can remember your pre-sleep intentions to cultivate experiences within dreaming's safe confines—including experiences that may not be accessible to you while you're awake.

The environments in which these dreams play out can appear as lifelike to you as the waking world, and are often accompanied by fantastical beauty, extravagant colors, a vivid heightening of the senses, and bliss. All of this occurs during a restful state of sleep.

A moment of lucidity, for example, may appear during a nightmare when you suddenly realize that you're actually safe in bed, so you wake yourself up. Or perhaps—once lucid—you recognize the chance to defy physical laws of the universe—experiencing the exhilaration of flying as freely as a bird.

EXPLICIT AWARENESS

Lucid dreaming is, first and foremost, knowing that you're dreaming. But to say that you know you are dreaming you must pay regard to the fact that there are many different types of knowing. In the case of lucid dreaming, the knowing that you are dreaming is *explicit*, which means that it can be easily articulated: You can spell out, "I am dreaming" while in the dream state, which is not something that you do when you are usually dreaming, a state henceforth referred to as *nonlucid dreaming*. This ability to directly label your state as a dream is the ingredient that dramatically shifts your state of consciousness.

CREATIVITY, NOT CONTROL

Contrary to common belief, lucidity does not mean that you are controlling your dream. Controlling dream content isn't what lucid dreaming is actually about. But lucidity does empower you to change how you relate with and influence your dream. You can step back from the false narrative that your dreaming mind was constructing and create a different reality instead.

You see, lucid dreaming is more about creativity than control. You realize that you no longer have to abide by social norms or be cautious of real-world consequences. You find that you have more choices available to prompt valuable experiences. While this might give you a greater sense of "control," it doesn't mean that lucid dreaming is about lording over your dream characters and commanding all experiences to conform to your will. Not only is a high degree of control in dreams not always possible, it's also unrealistic and unhelpful to try to control everything. Sometimes, in fact, acceptance or surrender—the complete opposite of control—is the response needed to achieve a happier result.

The Benefits of Lucidity

Even just recognizing that you're dreaming is, in itself, an incredible experience. In an epiphany moment, the narrative you were just assuming was real is revealed to be mere illusion. But the main benefit of lucidity involves increased access to preferred and helpful experiences, which offers endless rewards. Next, I'll describe some of the ways that you can apply lucid dreaming toward enhancing your health and happiness.

he ultimate experience of freedom. This

g that you can't be physically harmed and

'd consequences to your actions or the

starkly contrasts with how you ordinarily

your reality—whether you are awake or in a dream.

Understanding that you are completely safe inside the dream frees you to think differently and experience new possibilities. Personal growth is less likely without a sense of physical, social, and psychological safety, which are among your most basic human needs. When you recognize you are safe in lucid dreams, you are free to be your true self, explore, and learn new things. These freedoms often lead to higher forms of self-development.

IMPROVE CREATIVITY

Lucid dreaming is one of the most powerful states for exercising your creative flexibility. Creativity has long played a role in our ability to survive, compete, connect with others, and thrive on this planet. One thing that the art of lucid dreaming clearly demonstrates is how rigidity in your thinking confines your possible experiences. But when you know you are dreaming, your perspective expands, allowing you to test more creative solutions for meeting your needs and goals. This is one of the many ways that lucid dreaming can help you learn to adapt better to waking conditions as well.

RESOLVE NIGHTMARES

One of the clearest, most universal applications of lucid dreaming is its capacity to resolve nightmares, which symbolically represent the stresses we're dealing with in our waking lives. Instead of struggling with your nightmares, lucidity empowers you to reconcile your inner conflicts and form a more compassionate relationship with the parts of yourself that these nightmares represent. Through lucid dreaming, your nightmares can turn into your greatest allies, teaching you what you most need to know.

OVERCOME PROBLEMS AND FEARS

Lucid dreams are also a remarkable tool for problem-solving and confronting fears. If you are seeking insight into a particular challenge you are facing—be it related to a relationship, your occupation, working through emotions, or the need for clarity and direction at a crossroads in life—this can be precisely and intentionally explored through lucid dreaming. Additionally, the absence of social and physical restrictions allows you to rehearse behaviors in a safe environment, facilitating new ways of relating to yourself, others, and the world around you. For example, you could use lucid dreams to rehearse a challenging conversation you are anticipating, practice public speaking, conquer a phobia, or develop confidence in other realms that are relevant to your life goals.

HAVE FUN

While lucid dreaming, any imaginable experience becomes more available, including worldly indulgences. You could roam ancient Greece, revel in fantasy realms, or gratify your senses through exotic foods, sexual experiences, or the most beautiful music imaginable—all while knowing that the imagery is being orchestrated entirely from within your own mind. This sort of wish fulfillment is an important part of your path toward higher self-development, and will reinforce your motivation to keep practicing lucid dreaming. Research consistently associates lucid dreams with more positive emotions than nonlucid dreams, and people report that lucid dreaming has an invigorating effect on their mood that can last through the following waking day.

KNOW THYSELF

"Who am I?" is one of the pinnacle questions of human existence.

Dreams can help you answer it by mirroring back your innermost feelings, experiences, and mental states. These can be represented either symbolically or transparently in your dream imagery. By improving your lucid dreaming skills, you can learn to be more accurate in your observations of yourself, and gain deeper insight into the workings of your mind. Contemplation and introspection by way of lucid dreaming are powerful ways to unveil core truths about yourself.

Lucid dreaming also lends scientists a breakthrough tool for understanding the nature of consciousness. Among humanity's biggest mysteries are how the mind and physical matter are connected, and how the brain produces conscious experiences. In lucid dreams, our minds are capable of producing awake-like conscious experiences, with one key exception: There is no external source of input from the physical world informing our dream models of reality. This is why experiments that are conducted with specially trained lucid dreamers can pave new avenues for separating the sources of consciousness, and progress our species' understanding of who we really are.

TRANSCEND

Transcendence is a multifaceted concept, but in simple terms, it means to go beyond the self, or the ordinary limits of reality. It implies connecting with something greater than the self, such as collective humanity, the universe, nature, or the divine. Transcendent experiences can help us overcome limited ideas about reality. They take place on a multitude of levels and often have spiritual connotations. Unbounded by the limits of the waking physical world, lucid dreams are known to serve as a bridge to these higher states of consciousness.

TIBETAN DREAM YOGA

Of the many cultural practices that have integrated dreams into their spiritual and religious viewpoints, Tibetan Buddhist Dream Yoga is best known for its substantial overlay with lucid dreaming. This complex discipline has been practiced for more than a millennium, and aims toward achieving a transcendental purpose.

You might be familiar with the term "yoga" from classes you have taken where you stretch your mind and body, hold postures, meditate, and work with your breath. While dream yoga does include some of these elements, there's more to it.

Dream yoga leads to profound realizations that waking reality and the after-death state are the substance of dreams. Dream yoga uses lucid dreaming to rehearse for life and death, as a means to liberate oneself from attachments that cause suffering, and as a path toward spiritual awakening.

Many dream yoga techniques overlap with how Westerners typically access and use the lucid dreaming state: Both involve recognizing you are dreaming, willfully changing elements of the dream, and working with fear and suffering. Like dream yoga practitioners, lucid dreamers from the West often use lucidity to enhance their waking lives, and deepen their understanding of how waking reality is as much of a mental construction as dreaming. Western perspectives are also capable of supporting deep spiritual exploration through lucid dreaming, so you don't have to know much about Tibetan Buddhism or dream yoga to have a spiritual focus in lucid dreams.

CONTINUED

TIBETAN DREAM YOGA continued

However, a key difference between Western and Tibetan practices of lucid dreaming is the fact that Tibetan Dream Yoga weaves lucid dreaming into its own cultural and spiritual belief systems, which are not well-understood by Westerners today. In the West, lucid dreaming is not encased in such a rich, culturally supportive container. This can make Tibetan Dream Yoga quite different from how you might understand or practice lucid dreaming yourself.

Begin at the Beginning

Like learning any new skill, the ability to reliably lucid dream requires patience and time to develop—and everyone progresses at their own pace. While not everyone has a penchant for lucid dreaming, you can be trained if you have the right attitudes. If you are motivated to lucid dream, you can learn to use effective induction practices consistently and correctly, which will increase how often you can dream lucidly.

While there are no clear-cut benchmarks differentiating levels of skill in lucid dreaming, the following should give a basic idea of what to expect as your lucid dreaming practice elevates from beginner to expert level. As your skill level advances, so should the frequency and quality of your lucid dreams.

> "Begin at the beginning, and go on till you come to the end: then stop."
>
> **—LEWIS CARROLL,** *ALICE'S ADVENTURES IN WONDERLAND*

THE BEGINNER

As a beginner, you may not recall ever having had a lucid dream, or perhaps you've only experienced brief moments of lucidity. This is the point at which it can be helpful to rely on others for clear instructions to induce lucidity. It can be harder for beginners to know how to filter out misinformation from what truly can help them lucid dream, but using reputable sources can help you learn faster and easier. Beginners are also more prone to becoming over-whelmed if they try to master a lot of skills too quickly—therefore, it's important to have realistic expectations and learn at a pace that works for you. Many motivated beginners learn how to induce lucidity with relative ease, often having a lucid dream soon after learning about the techniques. In other cases, it can take longer.

THE EXPERIENCED

Once you begin to experience more lucid dreams, your understand-ing of how to access and maintain the state will grow. You'll start to recognize the varying complexities of lucid dream situations, and how best to alter your approach to overcome obstacles. You may start to experience an increased ability to direct the dream and accomplish pre-intended goals, but there still may be areas where you lack focus or awareness about how to apply lucidity productively. Your skills will advance as you start to be able to use your outcomes and mistakes to improve the decision-making in your practice.

THE PROFICIENT

With accumulating experience, practice, and training, you'll achieve consistently higher levels of performance in lucid dreams. Being proficient in lucid dreaming means that you know the best steps to follow in most situations, that your practices are well-planned, and that you can deliberately accomplish intended actions during lucid dreams. You have a solid, broad repertoire of skills that lets you explore lucid dreaming with greater flexibility and ease, including applying your other forms of knowledge within the lucid dream state, such as spiritual practices or martial arts. High-level proficiency is attainable but uncommon, and it's not necessary to mature to this level of skill to develop a fulfilling lucid dream life.

THE EXPERT

Experts in lucid dreaming are extremely rare. Their practice is characterized by at least a decade of intense dedication, long training hours, and mentorship by other, more advanced experts. The lucid dreams of experts tend to have higher levels of lucidity, meaning that they demonstrate a fuller understanding of the implications of knowing that they are dreaming, and can create their preferred outcomes. Experts aren't perfect at lucid dreaming—they still encounter obstacles as they work to refine their practice. Your expertise in lucid dreaming can improve as you're able to integrate multiple knowledge disciplines into your understanding of the state, such as neuroscience, psychology, the arts, or other fields. Spiritual figures tend to display the highest order of mastery.

Pioneers of Lucid Dreaming

Discussions of lucid dreaming have been documented since the times of Aristotle. Early references, however, pale in comparison to the elaborate disciplines surrounding lucid dreaming recorded just a few hundred years later in the Tibetan Buddhist traditions. In the modern West, the most significant contributions to our realm of knowledge about lucid dreaming come from researchers of the 19th and 20th centuries.

MARQUIS D'HERVEY DE SAINT-DENYS

In the 19th century, lucid dreaming inquiries ranged from detailed descriptions of the lucid dream state to skepticism of its existence. The most influential work during this time came from the French scholar Marquis d'Hervey de Saint-Denys, who extensively recorded his dreams and did experiments while lucid.

In 1867, he published *Dreams and How to Guide Them*, which covers how to increase dream recall, induce lucidity, and direct dream events. Praised for its in-depth study of lucid dreaming, the book inspired 20th-century scholars including Frederik van Eeden, Celia Greene, Patricia Garfield, Jayne Gackenbach, Paul Tholey, and Stephen LaBerge, who further popularized the topic.

STEPHEN LaBERGE

Although the world had been aware of lucid dreaming for at least thousands of years, little was known about how to scientifically study and access the state until the work of the American psychophysiologist Stephen LaBerge. Even after the 1953 discovery of rapid eye movement (REM) sleep, the stage of sleep when you vividly dream, lucid dreaming was neglected as an area of study because scientists didn't believe that REM sleep could support the level of cognition needed for lucid dreaming. This skepticism was reinforced by the rarity of lucid dreams, and the difficulties in inducing and studying them in the laboratory, so they were dismissed as a form of daydreaming.

In 1981, LaBerge introduced the world to a new paradigm for studying consciousness. Since your eyes are not paralyzed during REM sleep, he showed that subjects could move their eyes in a predetermined pattern to communicate when they were lucid. People were now able to time-stamp lucid dream events as they conducted experimental tasks, giving scientists the ability to probe dreaming consciousness with an "inside view."

LaBerge developed induction methods that are widely used today, which have also made the state more available for research. These methods include the mnemonic induction of lucid dreams (MILD), the sleep interruption technique, methods for falling asleep consciously, and substances and technologies that can cue lucidity.

Despite the cold academic climate and disappearance of funding for dream studies, he devoted decades to more research while defending his work to peers, carving the path for mainstream science to eventually accept lucid dreaming. Thanks to his unremitting dedication to the science of lucid dreaming, we now have a strong basis for understanding lucid dreams—and the best ways to induce them.

PAUL THOLEY

The German gestalt and sports psychologist Paul Tholey also made significant contributions to the field of lucid dreaming through the 1980s. Similar to LaBerge, he developed methods for critically reflecting on one's state of consciousness and increasing people's ability to realize that they're dreaming.

He published papers on practicing motor skills during lucid dreams, as well as investigating consciousness in dream characters. He made noteworthy contributions to the mental health applications of lucid dreaming by demonstrating how to interact with the lucid dream world and its characters to create greater freedom of choice and therapeutic healing.

Tholey's research showed that lucidity can resolve nightmares via a change in attitude and behavior, once the dreamer realized the safety and malleability of the dream state. Unfortunately, much of Tholey's work has not yet been translated from German.

THE STANFORD SLEEP LAB

LaBerge began to study lucid dreaming as part of his PhD program in psychophysiology at Stanford University in 1977. His refinement of induction science allowed him to investigate hundreds of lucid dreams in the laboratory. In doing so, he demonstrated that lucid dreams occur primarily during REM sleep, and under conditions of increased nervous system activation.

LaBerge is known for many studies showing correspondence between dreamed and waking actions. In addition to showing that eye movements can be purposefully controlled during REM sleep, he showed that subjects can intentionally change their breathing patterns while dreaming. They can even communicate, albeit unreliably, in Morse code through dreamed fist clenches that were observed externally as muscle twitches.

Following his work at Stanford, LaBerge established the Lucidity Institute to continue researching and teaching lucid dreaming. His unique contributions to the field continue to play an instrumental role in what is known about lucid dreaming today.

Dream Science

Lucid dreaming itself is a vast subject, but it's encased in the even broader study of dreaming. Dreams have long inspired philosophers, poets, religious leaders, and artists to contemplate their meaning and reason for being. But recent advances in the neuroscience of sleep have brought on a host of new insights.

WHY WE DREAM

Why do we dream? The reason remains unknown, although there are a number of theories.

REM sleep, the stage of sleep when you dream the most, is thought to play a vital role in brain maturation and functioning. Newborns spend more time in REM sleep, which reduces with age as their brains mature—this suggests that REM sleep plays a critical role in learning and brain development.

When you go to sleep after a period of sleep deprivation, you will experience more REM sleep than usual. This is known as the "REM rebound" effect, and also suggests a functional need for dreaming.

Researchers have proposed that we evolved dreaming to give us a way to rehearse responding to threats in a safe environment, thus increasing our chances of survival in the real world. REM sleep has also been linked with memory and learning, creative problem-solving, and emotional processing.

WHY WE FORGET DREAMS

All human beings dream nightly, even if they do not remember it. Unless you make efforts to remember your dreams, you are prone to forget them quickly after waking. You are inclined to forget your dreams in similar ways that you are inclined to forget much of your waking experiences. Human memory functions as a space saver. Few, specific details from your day-to-day end up being stored in your long-term memory, because it would not have helped human beings survive on this planet if their state of consciousness were crowded with useless memories. Therefore, your brain attempts to assimilate the most important information from your experiences into your mental models of the world.

This automatic filtering of knowledge helps you learn new things, experience clarity in your thinking, and get your needs met in life. Memories that are not important are discarded, or if they are stored in the brain, they are made less accessible to normal conscious awareness.

Still, dream memories evaporate more quickly than waking memories. The precise reason for this is not fully understood. Your brain's chemistry and electrical activity during sleep likely hinder dreams from being easily remembered after waking. People with lower dream recall also tend to wake up less during the night, which also hints that how the brain is selectively activated during sleep predisposes you to forget nocturnal experiences. We also tend to remember experiences that have more personal relevance. This could explain why incoherent, bizarre, or unemotional dreams are less likely to be remembered than dreams with more organized, meaningful, or intensely emotional narratives. Moreover, modern culture doesn't encourage our natural abilities to remember dreams. Rather, you are conditioned to place more value on waking experiences, dismissing dreams as unimportant or meaningless reveries of the mind to be forgotten. Dream recall can easily be improved through motivation and intention, so your bias toward forgetting dreams can also be considered a learned behavior.

DREAMING AND REALITY: IT'S ALL THE SAME TO YOUR BRAIN

During REM sleep, your brain cuts off external sensory input and constructs a model of the world based on psychological determinants, including your expectations, interpretations, memories, and preconceptions about reality. While awake, your experience of consciousness is simulated in a similar way, with one exception: Your model of reality is additionally informed by sensory input from the material world. In other words, perception in dreams operates just like it does when you are awake, except that the imagery you perceive is not influenced by external sources.

Motor outputs are also cut off during REM sleep, presumably to prevent you from acting out your dreams, but dreamed actions are still represented in brain activity in similar ways that waking actions are. To your brain, doing something in a dream is just like doing it while awake.

LaBerge illustrated this through one of his classic studies, which examined eye movements as a measure of brain activity. Normally, when you visually track a moving object in the waking state, your eyes show a smooth pattern of pursuing the motion. But if you track a moving object in your imagination, your eye movements show a spiky, erratic pattern, since there's no clear visual stimulus to track.

In a study he conducted using highly skilled lucid dreamers, LaBerge compared motion perception across waking, dreaming, and imagined states by telling his subjects to extend an arm in front of them, then trace a large circle with the arm while fixing their gaze on the finger. When the task was performed in lucid dreams, the subjects' eye movements closely resembled how smoothly the eyes would move if they really were watching a moving object in the waking world. This is among a number of studies supporting that "seeing" and "doing" while you're dreaming work similarly in the brain as those functions do while you're awake.

DO DREAMS HAVE MEANING?

You may have wondered whether your dreams contain meaning about you or your life. Of course, we humans have turned to our dreams for meaning throughout history. Prior to the past couple of centuries, theories about what dreams mean revolved mainly around religious philosophizing.

It was only later that dream meanings were proposed to have psychological origins by Sigmund Freud, the Austrian neurologist who is known today as the father of psychoanalysis. Freud believed that dreams have bizarre, incoherent features because they disguise unacceptable wishes, repressed emotions, and unconscious inner conflicts. Though many modern approaches to dreams have since deviated from Freud's views, they still advocate that dreams do in fact contain helpful information, which can be explored for creative and therapeutic purposes.

There are also those who dismiss dreams from having any personal significance. This is not far from the theory put forth in the late 1970s by J. Allan Hobson, an American psychiatrist and sleep researcher. His ideas reduced dreams to meaningless by-products of human neurobiology. Hobson proposed that dreams were the result of cells randomly firing in the lowest, most primitive level of your brain—the brain stem—during REM sleep, making dreams devoid of any original meaning. The higher parts of your brain, he proposed, receive this electrical and chemical noise and synthesize it into bizarre, haphazard stories.

Hobson's theory is incongruent with research showing that dreams do have coherent themes that reflect real concerns, emotions, and experiences from waking life. He also disregards the fact that REM sleep can support top-down control from your brain's higher thinking centers, ignoring studies demonstrating that logical reasoning, volition, and self-reflection are present in nonlucid and lucid dreams in similar ways as when you're awake.

The balance between meaning and meaninglessness has long been a part of our existential dialogue. There is still much to be discovered about the psychological and physical determinants of reality, and the role of meaning-making in producing consciousness. Though we don't yet have a fully assimilated view of the meaning of dreams, it's obvious that by trying to understand them, we can better learn to understand ourselves and how our minds work.

DREAM INTERPRETATION

There are many ways of trying to understand your dreams. You might try to read into possible meanings through their metaphors, idioms, or puns, or you can parallel your dream imagery directly to aspects of your life.

If you're trying to get somewhere in your dream, you might consider how that imagery parallels a path that you're pursuing in your waking life. Or if you dream that there are insects dancing atop your head, consider what might be on your mind that's bugging you—and then use that information to enhance insight and self-understanding.

Dream interpretation isn't the same as lucid dreaming, nor is it a requirement to lucid dream. However, finding meaning in your dreams can be an incredibly enriching complement to your lucid dreaming practice. If you understand what something in a lucid dream represents, you can learn how to change the dream for the better.

What to Expect

The program outlined in this book provides a path to begin lucid dreaming, giving you a strong foundation to grow on. Each chapter presents new skills that will help you develop the optimal mind-set for lucid dreaming.

OVERVIEW OF CHAPTERS

Chapter 2 will prepare your mind for learning the techniques that trigger lucid dreams, and also provide information that will help you plan out how and when you will practice skills. Chapter 3 will train you to develop your memory for recognizing the dream state, and set up the ideal mind-body conditions for lucid dreams. In chapter 4, we consider what to do to sustain and apply lucidity effectively, and it provides activities to explore. Chapter 5 points you in directions for growing your practice. Learning lucid dreaming can be quite simple, but at the same time, it also has its complexities. Since all the tools at your disposal can be a lot to remember, I have provided chapter 6 as a quick reference guide so that you can see what it would look like should you choose to implement a full protocol of induction skills in a single 24-hour period.

PRACTICE POINTS

To get the full benefit from this book, aim to do the recommended Practice Points regularly. They're designed to give you simple, structured tasks that will improve your ability to learn through direct experience.

LUCID DREAM REPORTS

One of the challenges that has kept the field of lucid dreaming from advancing further is that claims about lucid dreaming are often not substantiated with examples of direct experiences. Although no single dream report can prove anything about lucid dreaming, it can give an idea as to what is possible and highlight lucid dreaming's complex and varied nature. To give more of a glimpse into the range of possible experiences, this book includes examples of real lucid dreams—many are my own, though some come from my clients or students, cloaked for privacy.

Toward Lucidity

No construct of consciousness is easily boxed into neat categories. However, by having a working definition of lucid dreaming, and by naming some worthy pursuits to explore in this state, we as dreamers can access an abundance of new pathways for understanding and influencing reality.

Historically, it should be noted, lucid dreaming is embedded in non-Western disciplines. But thanks to modern science, today's researchers have been able to verify its existence and identify a set of practices, tools, and technologies that are capable of yielding more access to this rich state of being.

Current science proposes that dreams play a critical role in human maturation and functioning. Lucid dreaming, no less, has the potential to play an adaptive role in the very evolution of consciousness. With the key difference between dreaming and waking perception being external sensory input, the lucid dream state offers a favorable environment to rehearse for living—and, according to Tibetan Buddhist Dream Yoga, for dying as well.

Lucid dreaming is not the same as dream interpretation. However, the meaning with which you imbue your nightly imagery can inspire even greater reward, motivation, and commitment as you pursue this extraordinary state of consciousness.

CHAPTER 2

PRELIMINARIES TO LUCID DREAMING

To prepare you to learn how to induce lucid dreams, this chapter will guide you toward a better understanding of your sleep, and toward setting goals for exploring lucidity. We'll cover the stages of sleep you transition through every night, which will eventually help you plan your lucid dream induction techniques. You'll also get tips for optimizing your sleep habits.

It should be pointed out, however, that being able to remember your dreams is the main starting point for learning how to lucid dream. With that in mind, this chapter teaches you how to develop a high degree of dream recall. That way, you can be familiar with the scenarios in which you'll be intending to realize that you're dreaming. Since dream recall is best cultivated by writing dreams down, you'll also get suggestions for journaling your dreams.

While strengthening your dream-recall abilities, you should also be preparing your mind for what you would like to explore in your next lucid dream. The end of this chapter will guide you on how to clarify which goals you'd like to accomplish in the lucid dream world, while still remaining open to its wonderful spontaneity.

Understanding the Four Stages of Sleep

In a typical night, you cycle through four stages of sleep that are divided into two categories: Rapid Eye Movement (REM) and non-REM sleep. During non-REM sleep, you progress from light sleep (N1) to deeper and deepest sleep (N2 and N3, respectively). Then you cycle back from deep to light sleep and have your first period of REM sleep. A single cycle repeats several times over the night, about every 90 minutes for the average person, though this length of time can vary. Multiple brief awakenings from sleep are common and normal to experience throughout the night.

Figure 2.1: Hypnogram Example

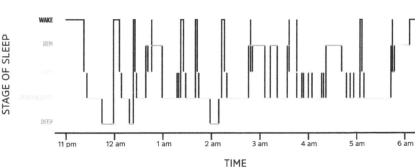

Above: Stages of sleep in a 31-year-old male. Courtesy of Lucidity Sleep & Psychiatry, San Diego, CA.

RAPID EYE MOVEMENT (REM) SLEEP

The REM stage is most associated with dreaming and lucid dreaming. Dreaming is possible during other stages of sleep, but compared to non-REM sleep, you are most likely to remember being fully immersed in a vivid, narrative-driven experience when you are awakened from REM sleep. When you measure brain activity during REM sleep, the pattern looks similar to wakefulness; this stage is nicknamed *paradoxical sleep* because your brain appears to be awake even though you're sleeping.

Many factors play a role in how much REM sleep you'll experience. REM sleep reduces with aging and is suppressed with certain medications and substances, like alcohol and marijuana. Conditions such as depression and other psychiatric disorders, as well as certain medications (acetylcholinesterase inhibitors used in the treatment of Alzheimer's disease, for example), can increase REM sleep.

The average adult cycles through four to five REM periods over a standard eight hours of sleep, accounting for about two hours total of REM sleep per night. Your REM periods are initially short but gradually lengthen toward the early morning. Though you can have lucid dreams in any REM period, it can help to focus your induction practices in the latter half of the night, when your REM periods are longer and more frequent. Estimating that you have a chance to lucid dream in REM sleep about every 90 minutes is a good rule of thumb.

LIGHT SLEEP (N1)

The N1 stage is known as "light" or "transitional" sleep, since it occurs as you transition from being awake to being asleep. This is when you gradually lose awareness of your external environment, and bodily functions like breathing and heart rate begin to slow. Most N1 sleep occurs during the first and last part of sleep, accounting for less than an hour of an average eight-hour night.

Hallucinations, known as hypnagogic imagery, can appear as a variety of visual and nonvisual images during your transition from being awake to light sleep. You can become aware of these images by deliberately paying attention to them. Hypnagogic images that are visual in nature may appear as though they're playing out on your closed eyelids, or within your mind's "eye." These may include swirling colors or geometric patterns, dark moving shadows, clear images of faces, or even whole scenes. It's also possible to perceive sounds, speech, or other sensations, like falling. Long, repetitive activities before sleep, such as playing video games or sailing through rhythmic ocean waves, can result in the hypnagogic state being dominated by similar imagery.

INTERMEDIATE SLEEP (N2)

More than half of your sleep is characterized by the N2 stage, known as "intermediate" sleep. During N2, your brain and bodily functions continue to slow. Both N2 and N1 sleep increase as you age, at the expense of REM and deep sleep.

DEEP SLEEP (N3)

N3 is known as "deep" sleep, which accounts for about an hour to 90 minutes of an average night's sleep. This stage mostly occurs in the beginning of the night, with little to no deep sleep during the latter half of your nightly sleep session. It's hardest to wake someone up from deep sleep. This important sleep stage plays a role in your immune system and stimulates the growth and restoration of bodily tissues. The older you grow, the less deep sleep you'll get. Substances like caffeine and alcohol also suppress deep sleep.

SLEEP PARALYSIS

During the REM stage of sleep, your muscles become paralyzed as your brain stops electrical and chemical signals from traveling to your body, a temporary condition called *sleep paralysis*. Everyone experiences sleep paralysis nightly, though most people aren't aware of it.

Becoming aware of sleep paralysis usually happens when you are either entering or exiting REM sleep. The state is completely harmless, although its features can seem bizarre or uncomfortable—you might experience your body in bed as feeling heavy and unable to move, as well as other unusual sensations (see page 64).

Outside of lucid dreaming, people with untreated medical disorders (like sleep apnea and narcolepsy) commonly experience sleep paralysis. It is also more likely during times of mental stress. Within a lucid dreaming practice, awareness during sleep paralysis can be deliberately induced, so that you can approach it with an attitude that helps you enter a lucid dream. Many lucid dream explorers find awareness during sleep paralysis to be enjoyable and fascinating.

Create Good Sleep Habits

Healthy sleep habits will give you more opportunity to dream, and to recognize that you're dreaming. Being fully rested will also ensure that you can focus your mind on the skills you need to employ for recognizing the dream state. Moreover, the art of lucid dreaming involves incorporating a bit of "wakefulness" into the night—meaning that practices can involve waking from dreams in the middle of the night to remember dreams and apply induction techniques. So it's important to establish behaviors that are conducive to falling asleep quickly and easily.

SLEEP HYGIENE

Here's a set of flexible guidelines for improving your ability to get sufficient, restful sleep.

Regulate light exposure. Light affects your biological rhythms that are responsible for daytime alertness and night-time restfulness. Get bright, early-morning sunlight every day, and dim your artificial lights late in the evening. Power down your electronics at least 30 to 60 minutes before bedtime.

Avoid caffeine and alcohol late in the day. Both of these substances negatively impact sleep quality.

Reserve your bed for only sleep or intimacy. Avoid engaging in wakeful activities in your bed, such as watching television or surfing the Internet. These activities condition your mind to be distracted and unfocused while in bed, which doesn't help you get restful sleep or focus inwardly on your dream life.

Wind down before sleep. Engage in a calming activity 30 to 60 minutes before sleep, like reading, grooming, or spending time with loved ones. Clear your mind and turn off the day's concerns.

By following these suggestions, you'll be giving your mind and body permission to restore themselves with the highest-quality sleep possible. This will help you perform at your best during the day, as well as support your ability to lucid dream.

PRACTICE RELAXATION

Quiet your mind as you fall asleep. Focus on feeling good about what you accomplished during the day, and avoid planning, worrying about the future, or thinking about the past. Keep a meditative focus on your breathing or relaxing your muscles, or imagine that you are in a peaceful nature scene to help you relax. Improving your relaxation skills will help you sleep better, and they can also play a role in some methods for inducing lucid dreaming.

LOOK FORWARD TO YOUR DREAMS

Most people don't consider the fantastical scenarios they will visit each night. As you lie in bed, be curious and eager for what your dreaming mind has to show you. Know, as you are going to sleep, that you'll soon experience several opportunities for becoming lucid and remembering your dreams.

Dream Recall

As mentioned earlier, good dream recall is a prerequisite for being able to lucid dream more often. So it's not surprising that people who lucid dream frequently are better at remembering their dreams. If your dream recall is low, you won't know what to focus on for becoming lucid. Though dream recall comes more naturally to some than others, it is easy to strengthen with the right mind-set—sometimes it can be as simple as intending to remember your dreams upon waking and writing them down. Here are some best practices for remembering your dreams.

PLAN TO REMEMBER

To embark on a successful lucid dreaming practice, you must plan out how you will remember your dreams. As you lie down to fall asleep, remind yourself that you're about to have several periods during which you'll be dreaming. Set an intention to wake up from, remember, and record these dreams.

NOTICE NOCTURNAL AWAKENINGS

In a normal night of sleep, you briefly awaken several times before quickly falling back asleep. These nocturnal awakenings are prime opportunities to remember and write down dreams. But you usually don't notice these awakenings, or you quickly forget them. Whenever you awaken in the middle of the night, remember to notice explicitly that you just woke up, and this is your chance to recall dreams. This strategy can help you develop an ability to remember several dreams in a given night of sleep, if desired.

WRITE DOWN YOUR DREAMS

Dream recall and writing down dreams go hand in hand. If you don't record your dreams, you are not likely to develop the high-level recall required to lucid dream as well as you'd like. The minute you wake up, record as many details as you can remember. The longer you wait to record your dream, the more likely it'll fade and be forgotten. It can help to make a habit of writing down something no matter what—even if you only remember a fleeting image, write it down.

LIE STILL

If your initial recall seems low when you wake, lie still with your eyes closed—don't move from your sleeping position and trace back your steps. By not moving, you can take advantage of your state-dependent memory, which is a type of memory that lets you retrieve memories better when you are in the same environment, or in this case, the same bodily position, that you were in when the memories were created.

JOG YOUR MEMORY

If you're having trouble remembering your dreams, consider the things that you tend to dream about. Ask yourself if any of those experiences, symbols, or themes were present in the specific dream that you're trying to remember. You may also jog your memory with categories of things that people tend to dream about. For example, go through types of settings, emotions, colors, or actions, such as walking, talking, or driving. Ask yourself if anything related to these categories was present in your dream. Alternatively, go through the alphabet as you lie in bed attempting to recall your dream. Ask yourself if anything in your dream started with an "A," "B," "C," and so on.

SET THE ALARM

If you sleep so deeply that you have little to no dream recall, you can improve your ability to remember your dreams with a strategy that uses an alarm clock. Here's how it works: Knowing that you have a REM period about every 90 minutes while you're sleeping, set an alarm to chime during the early morning hours when you are likely to be dreaming, for example, four and a half or six hours after you turn out the lights. Or you could set an alarm every 90 minutes to wake and ask yourself, "What was I just dreaming?" and apply other dream-recall strategies.

PRACTICE POINT: SET UP
DREAM RECALL

Tonight, before you sleep, set an intention to remember your dreams, and also to awaken from your dreams to write them down. Remind yourself that every 90 minutes or so, you'll be dreaming and be given this chance. Know, too, that you'll naturally experience several brief awakenings over the course of the night. Set your mind to explicitly notice when you wake up and then when you do, say to yourself: "I am awake now. What was I just dreaming?" Recall and record the dream in as much detail as you can.

Dream Journaling

To develop the high-level dream recall that you'll need to have for lucid dreaming, you'll need to start journaling your dreams often. Your dream journal will then become your chief reference guide for identifying the cues that you'll learn to associate with remembering that you're dreaming. It will also be valuable for enhancing your ability to derive meaning and inspiration from your dreams. This section, then, offers guidance on how to keep a dream journal.

EASY ACCESS

Keep your materials—pen, notebook, and light—beside your bed so that you can easily reach them whenever you wake up from a dream. Consider buying a pen that has a built-in light so that you won't have to turn on a lamp or flashlight. Alternatively, you can use a recording device or note-taking app on an electronic device.

KEYWORDS

You may find it tough to record all the details of your dreams every night. If you're short on time or energy, then at least record a few key bullet points about the dream, such as the main events, settings, people, or emotions. If you have a busy schedule, or so high a level of dream recall that it's impractical to write down all your dreams, just using keywords can help you keep a log of what your dreams are like. If you have a lower degree of recall and you are motivated to improve this skill, it'll serve you better to write down as many details as you can remember from as many dreams as possible.

HOW TO RECORD YOUR DREAMS

Organize your dream journal with a structured format so that you can efficiently record your dreams and glean important information from your nightly adventures. Here's a good outline for how to record dreams in your journal.

DATE: *Write down the date you had the dream.*

TITLE: *Give your dream a title, similar to how you'd title a poem or a movie. To help inspire it, think of the dream's essence. Titles can help you better remember previous dreams later and can also serve as a metaphor for the personal meaning underlying the dream.*

DREAM REPORT: *Here's where you record everything that you remember happening in your dream, in as much detail as possible. Include the sequence of events, all the people present, the setting, sensations, and your reactions.*

EMOTIONS: *Describe the emotions you had while dreaming, when they occurred, and why you think you felt that way. Awareness of inner states tends to be underreported unless you specifically focus on them. It's worth sharpening your awareness of the emotions from your dreams, since they can be useful cues for remembering you are dreaming in future dreams.*

THOUGHTS AND BELIEFS: *Identify the thoughts and underlying beliefs that you experienced during the dream. Since becoming lucid involves a shift in your thinking, it will help to enhance your awareness of your in-dream thinking patterns.*

POST-DREAM REFLECTIONS: *Jot down any reflections you had about the dream after you woke up. Some people use this section to interpret their dream's meaning, or for other musings and explorations.*

PRACTICE POINT: WRITE A DREAM JOURNAL ENTRY

Below is an example of a completed dream journal entry. This flexible format should help you consider how to structure your own journal entries to best support your awareness of your dreams.

DATE: *September 23*

TITLE: *Backseat Driver*

REPORT: *It's time to pick my son up from school. I get in my car but can't find my keys. The engine suddenly starts running, and I figure that my husband probably installed a keyless ignition without my knowing. The car seems really difficult to control, and I'm swerving into different lanes. I notice that I'm actually in the back seat of the car and I wonder why they make cars this way.*

EMOTIONS: *When I can't find my keys, I feel concerned that my son would not be happy if I was late. I feel fear when I am unable to control the car. I am confused about driving from the back seat.*

THOUGHTS AND BELIEFS: *Where are my keys? I don't remember my car having keyless ignition. Maybe my husband installed it for me. This car is out of control! I need to go to the repair shop. It's dangerous for the driver's seat to be in the back.*

POST-DREAM REFLECTIONS: *My car really does need some repairs, so this dream could be including some residue from my waking life. I also wonder if this dream is related to the disagreements I've had with my husband about how my son wants a later curfew.*

ADVENTURES IN LUCIDITY

I'm hiking alongside some steep, sunlit bluffs when I remember that I wanted to realize that I was dreaming. I recall, "This is my chance to fly!" I mentally will myself to hover, which, to my surprise, is easy. I start soaring through a golden, tree-lined canyon above a rushing stream. I am so filled with joy that I spontaneously begin shouting, "Thank you!" to the dream for letting me have such an incredible experience. When I land, a few dream characters approach to congratulate me for becoming lucid.

Set Your Lucid Dreaming Goals

Your time in lucid dreams is precious and often brief. There are endless options to explore, but if you don't plan ahead for what you'll do, the lucid dream may be over before you can derive anything valuable from it. To use your time wisely, set goals that include clear and specific tasks that you can carry out within the dream. You may not always be able to predict what will happen when you seek specific experiences in lucid dreams. But clearly defining your vision beforehand will increase your chances of success.

PLAN OUT SPECIFIC TASKS

In your journal, create a list of the goals that you want to achieve during your lucid dream state. Make each task specific and actionable. Avoid setting goals that are too vague, as in, "I just want to get lucid."

To help yourself brainstorm these tasks, reflect on the things that you value most in life. Set goals to explore your waking interests while lucid dreaming—be it art, spirituality, history, sports, relationships, meditation, or the nature of consciousness. Then think of a specific task that you can perform in a lucid dream to help you explore these areas.

You might also consider the things you'd like to do that would be impossible or less accessible in your waking life. Flying like Superman, for example, is an excellent and constructive task for beginners. Not only is it fun, but it will also give you a taste for how pliable your reality is when you deconstruct your waking assumptions.

At bedtime, choose one task that you'll remember to carry out if you do have a lucid dream. Remind yourself of your goal right before sleep, to increase your motivation and focus for achieving lucidity.

SAVE ROOM FOR SPONTANEITY

While it's best to have goals in mind, it's also important to allow room for spontaneously exploring the lucid dream world. So you'll want to balance your goal-setting with just being open to observing and exploring the lucid dream state without necessarily trying to change it. In fact, implementing a pre-intended task in a lucid dream could cause you to miss other elements in your dream that could have been interesting or helpful to explore. On the other hand, if you don't try to change your reality in some way, you won't see as much transformation. With time, you'll learn to balance these factors in ways that work for you.

"BIG DREAMS"

"Big Dreams," as defined by the 20th-century Swiss psychiatrist Carl Jung, emerge from something bigger than the self. He believed that Big Dreams arise from a deeper, broader layer of consciousness that is shared by all beings. These dreams are thought to be of a higher order and stand out for their profound meaning.

Lucid dreams will often leave you with feelings of awe and wonder. More rarely, a lucid dream could be so powerfully transformative that its meaning seems to transcend relevance to the person having the dream. These are the types of lucid dreams that tend to stick with you, feel larger than life, and have greater significance and connection to universal motifs. It's quite possible that the high level of awareness, recall, and purposeful volition that's afforded by lucidity makes these Big Dreams more accessible.

Gearing Up for Lucidity

By understanding your sleep stages and how to tend to your sleep quality, you will be more prepared to learn how to lucid dream. Remembering your dreams will be a pillar that supports your entire lucid dreaming practice, so write them down in a journal on a regular basis. You learned that having clear, predetermined goals in mind will help you best take advantage of your time lucid dreaming. To enhance your focus and motivation for inducing lucidity, remind yourself at bedtime of the specific task you plan to accomplish that night once you realize you are dreaming. In the next chapter, you will begin exploring techniques to induce lucid dreams.

CHAPTER 3

METHODS OF INDUCTION

To regularly and deliberately lucid dream, you'll need a clear plan for what to do and how to do it. Your success will be determined by how well you optimize two factors: "set" and "setting." "Set" refers to the knowledge, attitudes, and practices that you apply toward remembering that you're dreaming. "Setting" refers to your brain's physiological state.

The mind-set for lucid dreaming involves developing your ability to set and carry out intentions to do something specific: to recognize the dream state while dreaming. This is done by training yourself to identify the features that distinguish your dreams from waking reality—referred to as *dreamsigns*. Then your intentions to notice you're dreaming when you encounter dreamsigns are strengthened through memory exercises.

The other requirement for lucid dreaming is your brain's activational state. Lucid dreaming is most likely to take place during a highly activated form of REM sleep, when your sleeping brain is in its most wakeful state. These physiological opportunities for lucid dreaming occur several times over a normal night of sleep, with more frequency in the early morning hours. Certain methods can enhance your degree of "wakefulness"—how activated your brain is during REM sleep—including sleep interruption or galantamine, a memory-enhancing substance.

This chapter will guide you on how to develop an integrated repertoire of skills for inducing lucid dreaming. Take your time learning each skill, and add more to your repertoire once you build confidence in your abilities. Developing a sharp eye for explicitly recognizing the dream state may not happen overnight, but consistent practice and ongoing refinement of these tools will help you be on your way.

Dreamsigns

Dreams are full of features that distinguish them from waking reality. These features, known as dreamsigns, can serve as signals that you are dreaming. While dreaming, you don't ordinarily think about the uniqueness of your experiences. You simply accept what's presented as real. If you do happen to notice that a situation is odd, you're more likely to justify the experience rather than realize it's a dream. For example, if you notice a new, large crack in the foundation of your house, you might be quicker to reason that an earthquake must have created it rather than consider that you could be dreaming. Although you're biased to think this way in dreams, you can train yourself to think differently by strengthening your mental associations of dreamlike events with remembering that you're dreaming.

IDENTIFY DREAMSIGNS

Dreamsigns can be described as events that have a lower probability of occurring in waking life. They often appear in the form of something unusual or unlikely, if not impossible, in physical reality. For instance, you might dream that you're divorced when you're actually married, or that you're in a strange new place that's outside of the usual range of your daily routines.

From another angle, dreamsigns can be understood as events that have a higher probability of occurring in the dream state. In other words, these events are distinctly dreamlike or are highly characteristic of your own personal dream life. For example, you might often dream that you can't find something, such as your parked car or your hotel room. You may have difficulty remembering things as well as you usually would, like forgetting when you enrolled in a class. You may notice that you regularly experience certain emotions, like surprise or confusion, in your dreams, or that while dreaming, you often notice how peculiar something is.

To improve your awareness of dreamsigns, you'll need to regularly practice identifying them from your personal dreams. After you record a dream, highlight which elements in the dream were signs that you were dreaming. You can also make a list of all your dreamsigns in one place so you can review them periodically and get better at recognizing them in future dreams.

INTEND TO NOTICE DREAMSIGNS

Dreamsigns can be thought of as memory targets. Using intention-setting strategies, you target your dreamsigns as signals to remember that you're dreaming. The recurring quality of certain dreamsigns can be especially useful. Since you can reliably expect a recurring dreamsign to appear in the future, you can focus your mind to notice it the next time you encounter it during a dream.

Is it possible to spontaneously remember that you're dreaming without being cued by a dreamsign? Yes. However, your mind is constantly processing information from your environment, whether you're aware of it or not. Dreamsigns still prime the mind for lucidity, even if you weren't conscious of a precursor. It is more efficient to focus on noticing dreamsigns to cue lucidity, as opposed to trying to become lucid at some vague future point in time.

DREAMSIGN CATEGORIES

Dreamsigns present themselves in myriad ways. You can grow more astute at recognizing them by getting to know the underlying categories that tie their seemingly disparate features together.

LaBerge conducted a series of studies on the varying ways that dreamsigns appear. Then he condensed them into four categories: form, context, action, and inner awareness. "Action" and "inner awareness" were the dreamsign categories most likely to result in lucid dreaming. Dreams that contained more dreamsigns were also more likely to produce lucidity.

Table 3.1: LaBerge's Dreamsign Categories

CATEGORY	DESCRIPTION	EXAMPLES
Form	The shape of your dream body, other people, or objects is strange, morphing, deformed, or typical of your dreams. Familiar contexts or places may have abnormal features. Objects may disappear, or you may not be able to find something you're looking for.	*I'm getting the newspaper on my front porch, but when I turn around, my house is no longer there.* *The bottom of the stall door in a public bathroom is only the height of my chest.*
Context	You find yourself in a setting or situation that would be unlikely to occur in waking life, or one that you often experience in your dreams.	*I am in the kitchen of my childhood home.*

Table 3.1: LaBerge's Dreamsign Categories (continued)

CATEGORY	DESCRIPTION	EXAMPLES
Action	A single action or action sequence is strange or impossible in the physical world, or characteristic of your dreams. Technology tends not to function like it should.	*I'm pumping my car's brakes, but it's not working.* *I can still see perfectly even though I just removed my prescription glasses.*
Inner Awareness	Sensations in your body may be odd or different from your usual range of sensations, or characteristic of sensations that you often feel in dreams. You have thoughts that are odd or similar to the thoughts that you usually only experience while dreaming. Emotions are more intense or resemble the emotions you tend to experience while dreaming.	*My body feels heavy, like lead.* *I think to myself, "How odd!"* *I feel surprised to find that something is different than it usually is.*

Review your dream journal entries to identify the features in your dreams that are dreamsigns. Then create a list that logs all your dreamsigns in one place. Next to each dreamsign, write down whether it fits best in the form, context, action, or inner awareness category. Circle, underline, or highlight dreamsigns that tend to recur.

Make sure that you're identifying a balanced number of dreamsigns from all four categories. Sometimes a dreamsign will fit into more than one category, depending on what dimension of consciousness you're focusing on. In the classic dream in which you can't run because your legs are paralyzed, for example, the inability to move would be in the action category, while the heavy leg sensation would be in the inner awareness category.

Continue to add to this list as you recall more dreams. Remind yourself that the next time you encounter these or other dreamsigns, you'll remember that you are dreaming.

Mnemonic Induction of Lucid Dreams (MILD)

You already have the ability to effectively set and carry out intentions for the future. You use this form of memory frequently in your daily routines, for example, when you remember to call someone back or drop something in the mailbox. The Mnemonic Induction of Lucid Dreams technique, or MILD, is a prospective memory technique designed to help you set and carry out the intention to remember that you are dreaming. LaBerge developed this method during his dissertation research to increase willful access to the lucid dreaming state.

ADVENTURES IN LUCIDITY

I was having a series of dreams in which wolves were threatening me. I'd be staying in a cabin in the wilderness with friends when wolves would begin to surround our abode. Fearing for our safety, I would run, hide, or try to defend us.

When it became clear that these wolves were repeat visitors, I knew that I had to become lucid in my next dream of wolves and face them. Determined, I set my mind to realize I was dreaming the next time I encountered a wolf.

Sure enough, the wolves returned. I was sitting cozily near the fireplace with friends. The cabin became abuzz about a pack that was dashing toward us.

"Wolves?" I stood up with conviction. "This is a dream!"

A silver wolf charged through the door. It pounced on me as I welcomed it with open arms. I fell back in my seat as it nuzzled me sweetly. I petted it and thanked it for being there. It grew agitated, growling as I held its head in my hands. I offered comfort, softly stroked its ears, and asked, "How can I help you? What do you need from me?" It calmed down again, licking my hands and face.

I was elated that I was able to transform a series of stressful dreams into one that was peaceful and thought-provoking. To this day, the wolves have not returned as nightmare figures. I also became more aware of how wolf symbolism had begun to weave its way into my ongoing search for meaning and self-understanding in my waking life.

SETTING INTENTIONS THROUGH THE THREE Rs

Consider for a moment the multitude of ways you set intentions to complete future tasks in your daily life. You might simply tell yourself in words that you're going to do something later, perhaps even reminding yourself of this intention periodically over the day. Or you might visualize the steps it would take for you to successfully complete the task. You might also write out your plan.

Let's say that you want to remember to change one of your behaviors, such as forgetting to floss your teeth nightly. When you wake and realize that you didn't floss last night, you could mentally rehearse your nighttime routine to include remembering to floss, which makes it more likely that you'll remember the next night.

To strengthen your intentions to lucid dream, the MILD technique guides you through a series of steps to help you plan to notice that you're dreaming, and to accomplish a productive lucid dreaming goal.

MILD is ideally practiced at nighttime, when you wake from dreams and prior to returning to sleep. When you awaken from a dream, you memorize it and apply the intention-setting skill that is remembered best as the three Rs: rescript, rehearse, and remind. Repeat these as many times as necessary to feel confident that you can carry out your intention to remember you are dreaming when you return to sleep.

1. RESCRIPT: When you wake from a dream, decide how you would re-sequence your dream's events to include becoming lucid. Choose a point in the dream during which you recognize a dreamsign and say, "This is a dream." Next, rescript the rest of the dream as if you remained aware that you were dreaming and carried out a meaningful task.

2. REHEARSE: Imagine yourself back in the dream, except this time, experience the new, rescripted version in which you became lucid. Visualize yourself becoming lucid and what the rest of the lucid dream would have been like. Repeat this visualization as many times as needed to clearly see yourself back in the dream, remembering you are dreaming.

3. REMIND: Set a mental reminder that when you return to sleep and begin dreaming, you will remember that you are dreaming. Tell yourself, "I will become lucid when I am next dreaming. I might encounter a dreamsign similar to those in my previous dreams, or it might be a different type of dreamsign. Next time I'm presented with a dreamsign, I will remember that I'm dreaming." Focus on this intention as you are falling back asleep.

The MILD technique may also be practiced during daytime hours. Essentially, you continue to remind yourself of your intention to lucid dream tonight. You can practice rescripting your recent nonlucid dreams as though you realized you were dreaming, or you can even rescript a waking experience as though it were a lucid dream instead. You then rehearse the rescripted version in your imagination. Repeat this until you feel that your intention is firmly set.

MILD PRACTICAL TIPS

The essence of MILD is simple, yet it also has intricacies. This section includes a few more tips to help you better understand and apply this practice over the night.

When you are applying the three Rs during brief awakenings in the middle of the night, you might find that you fall back asleep before you are able to complete the exercise. To prevent this, prop yourself up in bed momentarily to practice the three Rs before you return to sleep.

If you are unable to remember a dream when you wake, you can still practice MILD. All you need to do is select one of your other recent dreams that you recall well and practice rescripting and rehearsing that dream as if it were lucid instead.

After rescripting and rehearsing a recent dream, you might mistakenly expect that the next dream you have when returning to sleep is supposed to be the same. However, this is rarely the case and not the purpose of MILD. Rather, MILD uses your own mind's imagery as a training ground to rehearse what it takes to notice you are dreaming, thereby strengthening your ability to execute on intentions to lucid dream.

Be meticulous during your practice drills of the three Rs. Practice them at least several times in a row. Rehearse becoming lucid in slow motion and at other times practice at a faster pace. Visualize all aspects of the dream as vividly as possible, particularly more subtle aspects, such as what you were thinking and feeling. Thoroughly revise the dream, not just by incorporating the view that you know you are dreaming, but also precisely how your thinking will shift to remember you are dreaming in the first place. The more clearly you are able to imagine becoming lucid using your own dream imagery, the more agile and effective you will become in attaining lucidity in all sorts of future dream scenarios. Instead of visualizing yourself becoming lucid, you can also make use of alternative or complementary methods to help you rehearse what it would be like to become lucid. For example, you can write down the rescripted versions of your dreams in your journal, or verbally describe in detail the new narrative that includes becoming lucid.

Although the aim of practicing the three Rs during nocturnal awakenings is to become lucid in your next dream period, you may not always be successful. However, practicing the three Rs is still valuable because you are putting in the required work to strengthen your mental set for recognizing dreamsigns. Be persistent, because the more you practice MILD, the more skilled you will become at it and the more prepared you will be to lucid dream at your next opportunity.

PRACTICE POINT: PRACTICE MILD OVER THE NIGHT

Since you have several REM periods per night you can practice the MILD technique multiple times in the same night. This can be especially helpful if you want to choose a single night to focus intently on becoming lucid. However, it's not necessary to apply MILD every time you wake up from a dream, or even every night. It is acceptable to take a relaxed approach to MILD, applying it only when you feel motivated to focus on your practice.

If you do want to maximize your practice of MILD however, here's a sequence that outlines what MILD practice looks like when fully implemented from the time you turn out the lights until you rise from bed in the morning.

1. AT LIGHTS-OUT:

    - Set up dream recall: Intend to notice when you wake up during the night, and to remember your dreams.
    - Apply the three Rs: Rescript and rehearse one of your recent dreams as if it was lucid. Remind yourself to remember that you're dreaming tonight, letting this intention be the last thing on your mind as you drift to sleep.

- Explicitly notice that you have just woken up, then memorize your dream. Record your dream's details in your journal.
- Apply the three Rs again: Rescript and rehearse the dream you just woke from as if it were lucid. If you don't recall the dream, use the most recent dream that you do recall instead. Remind yourself to remember that you're dreaming when you return to sleep.

3. AT RISE TIME:

- Recall your dreams and write them down.
- Apply the three Rs once more: Rescript and rehearse the last dream you remember as if it were lucid. Since you'll be rising to start your day, remind yourself that the next time you go to sleep, you'll remember that you are dreaming.

Reflect on Your Present State

During waking hours, you can continue to strengthen your mind-set for inducing lucid dreams by reflecting on your present state of consciousness. It's rare for most people to consider that they may be dreaming while they're awake. You assume that you're awake without thinking much about it, but it is this exact assumption that interferes with realizing that you're dreaming. Therefore, you need to learn how to question the deeply rooted assumption that you are awake. By practicing this regularly, you'll be more prepared to recognize when you actually are dreaming.

"AM I AWAKE?"

Right now, consider whether you are awake. If you believe you are awake, how do you know this is true? What is your rationale that makes you so sure that you are not asleep?

The best way to determine whether you are awake is to first consider if any dreamsigns are present. Do you notice anything odd or improbable happening? Are any of your recurring dream-signs around? Is there anything dreamlike related to the categories of form, context, action, or inner awareness?

Even if you don't notice any signs that you are dreaming at the moment, how can you truly know that you are awake? You are partial to believing you are awake even when you're not, and frequently miss noticing the cues that indicate you might be dreaming, even if you're looking for them. So how can you really trust this assumption that you are awake right now?

When asked this question, one reason people report assuming they're awake is because they can't perform impossible feats like flying or pushing their hand through a wall—what's commonly referred to as "state testing" or "reality testing."

A state test is a way to test your assumption that you are awake by eliciting a specific type of dreamsign. However, the outcomes of your actions in dreams don't always go as predicted and can be influenced by your expectations, making most state tests a faulty way to determine if you are dreaming.

For example, if you believe that you are awake, you might expect that your hand would not be able to pierce through a solid wall, making it less likely to work in your dream, and thus preventing you from realizing that you actually are dreaming.

In other words, sometimes state tests work and other times they don't, so it's not efficient to rely on them when you practice determining your state of consciousness. However, there is an exception to this, described next, known as "the rereading state test."

THE REREADING STATE TEST

While dreams can appear convincingly real, they still lack an external source of sensory information. Consequently, the images you perceive in dreams have fewer stable features than those in the waking world.

In dreams, some perceptions are consistently less stable than others—particularly the rereading of small printed text. LaBerge developed the rereading state test as a means of strengthening dreamers' certainty about their true state of consciousness. So if you read text in a dream, like a few words in a book, then look away and read the text again, the vast majority of the time, the text will change. These changes could occur in the actual words, the font, the text size, or the words could disappear altogether.

After you conclude that no dreamsigns are present and you believe you are awake, conduct a rereading state test to confirm your state. Read some text, look away at another object, and reread it. If it stays the same, reread it one more time—except this time, expect the text to change. According to LaBerge's testing, if you perform the rereading state test in a dream, the text will change 95 percent of the time.

The rereading state test should be practiced while awake a few times per day. This way, you can rehearse breaking down your assumptions that you're awake, preparing your mind to notice the next time you are dreaming. If you are dreaming but you miss noticing a dreamsign, doing the rereading state test can be a helpful fail-safe that alerts you to become lucid.

PRACTICE POINT: PRACTICE THE REREADING STATE TEST

To make the rereading state test work best, practice it in the context of the "integrated skills protocol," outlined below. Aim to determine your state of consciousness using this protocol at least 5 to 10 times per day, as well as during your dreams. Ideally, practice in situations where you notice something unusual, dreamlike, or if you think about dreams or lucid dreaming.

1. ASK, "AM I AWAKE?": Seriously consider whether you are awake or dreaming and determine whether dreamsigns are present. If you truly are dreaming and notice it, you don't need to continue with these steps and further confirm your state, because you already know you're dreaming. If you don't notice dreamsigns and believe you are awake, proceed to step 2.

2. **REREAD TEXT:** Memorize some small printed text that contains at least a few words. Fully look away at another object, then go back and reread the text. Determine whether the text changed in some way. If the text changed, recognize that you are dreaming and enjoy the lucid state. If the text didn't change, continue to the next step.

3. **REREAD TEXT AGAIN:** Look away from the text again, but this time, expect that the text will change when you reread it. Imagine how the text might be different, then reread it to determine whether it changed. If it changed, acknowledge that you are dreaming and implement a meaningful lucid dreaming goal. If the text stayed the same, you may conclude that you're awake, but continue to step 4.

4. **APPLY THE THREE RS:** Even though you're probably awake, consider what it would be like if you *were* dreaming right now. What sort of dreamsigns would be present? How might the text have changed when you went back to read it again? And what would you have done if you became lucid? Decide how you would **rescript** this moment as though you were dreaming, noticed a dreamsign, and accomplished a lucid dreaming goal. Then, briefly **rehearse** in your imagination what this would have looked and felt like. Finally, **remind** yourself to remember that you're dreaming the next time you are dreaming.

EXTERNAL REMINDERS

Some lucid dreamers help themselves remember to ask, "Am I dreaming?" during the day by using external reminders, like writing the question on a sticky note and putting it somewhere that's easily visible. While external reminders can serve as a stepping-stone to remembering to ask this question on your own, their usefulness is limited, because you can't bring them into the dream state with you. There is one exception to this, and it's related to technological aids to induction. During LaBerge's work at Stanford, he found that if he flashed lights over dreamers' eyes during REM sleep, the flashing lights were incorporated into their dreams. These dreamers were able to train themselves to recognize the flashing lights as dreamsigns to become lucid.

NOTICE "WAKING DREAMSIGNS"

Though the waking world is quite different from your dreams, it also has similarities. A "waking dreamsign" is when you observe something dreamlike in your waking environment. Waking dreamsigns come in a variety of forms, but they tend to have an unusual or unique quality to them. These events are improbable but not impossible in waking reality. You may also notice certain features of your daytime experiences that resemble your dreams. Here are a few examples of how waking dreamsigns might appear:

- You run into a friend that you haven't seen in years.
- Your cell phone is acting oddly, and you can't make a call.
- A street artist appears to defy the laws of gravity.
- Your neighbor's front door is painted a different color than usual.
- The person sitting behind you on the subway is dressed as a clown.
- During your daily walk, you notice that a park bench is in a different location.
- You experience a strong emotion.

Encounters with waking dreamsigns are ideal opportunities to strengthen your intentions for lucid dreaming. Even though you will ultimately conclude that you are awake, you should complete all the steps of the rereading state test (see page 57), albeit with minor modifications.

When considering your state, ask yourself, "Is this experience odd or dreamlike enough to indicate that I'm actually dreaming?" If not, examine your environment for other cues that would clearly signal that you're dreaming. If there are none, conduct a rereading state test to make sure that you're awake. Lastly, apply the three Rs: Rescript and rehearse your waking experience as though it were a lucid dream and you accomplished an intended goal. Then remind yourself to notice when you are dreaming tonight.

The Sleep Interruption Method

Lucid dreaming occurs during a phase of REM sleep when the brain is more awake and activated. Part of what makes techniques like dream journaling and MILD helpful is the fact that they can briefly extend your natural awakenings before returning to sleep. These brief periods of wakefulness increase your level of brain activation, which can help you lucid dream when you return to sleep. Extending a period of sleep interruption can make lucid dreaming even more likely when you fall back asleep.

The sleep interruption method involves getting out of bed after about your third REM period, staying awake for 30 to 60 minutes, then returning to bed and practicing MILD until you fall back asleep. This method is sometimes referred to as "wake-back-to-bed." It's possible to estimate when you are experiencing your third REM period by knowing that you dream about every 90 minutes—you can then set an alarm to wake you up about four and a half hours after you turn out the lights. If you've been making sure to notice your nocturnal awakenings in order to recall your dreams, it is possible to learn to remember your first three dreams of the night and estimate more precisely when your third REM period will occur.

The activity performed during the sleep interruption period should be stimulating enough to wake you up, but not so stimulating that it will be difficult for you to go back to sleep—good suggestions include reading about lucid dreaming or writing in your dream journal.

Sleep interruption is a powerful strategy when combined with the proper mental set for lucid dreaming. Try incorporating a sleep interruption period into nights when you feel able to put a strong focus toward inducing a lucid dream.

It should be noted that though sleep interruption can increase your odds, it's not necessary to interrupt your sleep to have lucid dreams.

GALANTAMINE

In combination with the techniques described in this chapter, there's another option for inspiring lucidity. Available over the counter or by prescription, galantamine is a substance that belongs to the cholinesterase-inhibitor class of drugs. It works by temporarily increasing your natural levels of acetylcholine, a neurotransmitter that's essential to memory and regulating REM sleep. It is most commonly prescribed for people with dementia, who have a deficit in acetylcholine levels.

Since acetylcholine increases the intensity of REM sleep, and since lucid dreaming is known to occur in an intensely activated form of REM sleep, LaBerge reasoned that substances like galantamine could improve access to the lucid dream state when combined with the MILD and sleep interruption techniques.

We tested this with 121 volunteers attending LaBerge's intensive retreats (LaBerge, LaMarca, and Baird, 2018). At baseline, the group members had an average of four lucid dreams per year. After being trained in induction methods, participants took 8 mg, 4 mg, or 0 mg (placebo) of galantamine over three consecutive nights. They took their capsules after approximately the third REM period, then got out of bed for 30 minutes of wakefulness. After returning to bed, they practiced MILD until they fell back asleep for a nap.

Over the three nights, 57 percent of participants induced one or more lucid dreams on the nights that they took galantamine, compared to just 14 percent of participants who took the placebo. Though both doses were more effective than the placebo, the 8-mg dose was more effective than the 4-mg dose at stimulating lucid dreams. This showed that a combination of MILD, sleep interruption, and galantamine substantially increases your odds of lucid dreaming. (Note that the group's baseline rate of lucid dreaming still improved on nights that they took the placebo, showing that it's possible to improve lucid dreaming abilities without the use of galantamine.)

Galantamine's risk of adverse effects is low, mainly including mild stomach upset or trouble sleeping. However, galantamine can be risky for those with asthma, heart problems, stomach ulcers, or other conditions, and could interact negatively with other substances, such as blood pressure medications. As with starting any new supplement or medication, consult your doctor if you wish to explore galantamine for lucid dreaming.

Wake-Initiated Lucid Dreaming (WILD)

Most often, lucidity occurs in the middle of an ongoing dream when you have the insight, "I'm dreaming!" This type of lucidity onset is known as Dream-Initiated Lucid Dreaming (DILD). However, it is also possible to initiate lucidity directly from the waking state, known as Wake-Initiated Lucid Dreaming (WILD).

During WILD experiences, there's little to no lapse in awareness of your state of consciousness as you transition from waking to dreaming. You are lucid as soon as the dream begins. Often, this happens after a brief awakening from and immediate return to REM sleep. WILDs can also be induced in combination with the sleep interruption technique described previously.

Learning the common features of WILDs will help you learn to induce them. Generally, you progress from lying awake in bed to falling asleep and being embedded within a dream scene, all while fully aware of your state of consciousness.

In other WILDs, the exact point at which you begin to dream isn't as clear. Instead of suddenly being pulled into a distinctly new dream scene, you begin to dream that you're lying in bed trying to fall asleep. That is to say, you have a dream body in a dream bed in a dream bedroom. This transition from wake to sleep can be so gradual that you might not notice it, believing you're still awake when you're already dreaming.

THE WAKE TO REM SLEEP TRANSITION

Signs that you are consciously crossing the wake-sleep boundary can include sensory experiences that can seem bizarre. These are a normal, harmless, and fascinating part of consciously falling asleep. These experiences may include:

Sleep Paralysis

It is common to witness your body enter sleep paralysis (see page 31) when you're attempting to induce a WILD. You may be unable to move your limbs or speak, and your body may seem frozen. Being aware during sleep paralysis is completely safe and temporary, lasting only seconds or minutes. Keeping a positive attitude during sleep paralysis is important because the resulting imagery will mirror your emotions. If you're scared, you could experience fearsome or distressing imagery. If you're open and curious, your experience will be more interesting, comfortable, and pleasant.

Odd Bodily Sensations

You may sense tingling in your limbs or feelings of size distortion in your hands or feet. As you transition from wake to sleep, you might feel itchy, pulsating, or intense vibrations. You might also have kinesthetic hallucinations like walking, rocking, slowly descending, or falling—these all signal that you're close to the lucid dream state. One of the most commonly reported experiences when people are aware during the wake-sleep transition is the feeling of pressure or weight on the chest. This is because you lose muscle tone when you enter REM sleep (except for the muscles relevant to breathing and eye movements) and, in effect, the body collapses onto itself. This leaves mainly your diaphragm active to maintain your breathing, translating into an exaggerated feeling of chest compression as you continue to breathe without the aid of accessory breathing muscles, especially if you're lying on your back.

Visual Hypnagogic Imagery

If you're observing the sleep-wake transition, you can see images even though your eyes are closed. You might see moving figures or shapes in the darkness, or an entire dream scene may appear as though it's on a movie screen before you. It may seem that you can perceive your room, even though your eyes are shut. Sometimes these images fade as soon as you notice them. Other times, their clarity increases until you suddenly find yourself within a full scene of a dream.

Auditory Hallucinations

A normal part of WILDs is hearing unusual sounds. You might hear the whirring of a fan when there is none. You might hear a screeching sound, music, or talking that sounds like it's coming from a radio, TV, or someone else in the room.

A Presence in the Room

During the wake-sleep transition, it may seem like you're not alone. You might hear someone breathing next to you or taking steps down the hall. If you're still in bed but notice a visitor, it is likely that you have fully transitioned from waking to dreaming. You may consider interacting with the figure, or you could go explore an alternative lucid dream activity.

Abstract Thoughts

As you progress from wake to sleep, you might notice your mind wandering toward abstract or dreamlike thoughts.

HOW TO INDUCE WILD

Because the latter half of your sleep cycle is richer in REM sleep, focus on inducing WILD in the early morning hours. A good time to attempt WILD is after a planned 30- to 60-minute period of sleep interruption after your third REM period. You may also be able to induce WILD when you spontaneously awaken from the middle of a dream and immediately return to sleep. It may be possible to induce WILD during a daytime nap, but depending on the length of the nap and other factors, it's not guaranteed that you'll enter REM sleep.

Inducing WILDs involves using meditation, visualization, and other concentration methods for consciously observing the transition from waking to dreaming. The following is a sampling of techniques that can help you stay aware of your state while you fall asleep.

Mantras and Counting

To initiate lucidity directly from the waking state, you might concentrate on repeating a word or phrase as you fall asleep. For example: "I will remember that I am dreaming."

Counting yourself to sleep is also a technique that works well. Count "One . . . I will know when I'm dreaming, two . . . I will know when I am dreaming, three . . ." and so on.

As you count or repeat your selected phrase, you might notice your mind getting distracted or losing count. As soon as you notice this, bring your attention back. Know, though, that losing focus or count are good clues that you're getting more relaxed and closer to the dream state. When you notice this, rouse yourself just enough to maintain awareness of your state while continuing to drift into your dream.

Meditation

Meditation can help you transition into WILD by giving you a relaxed yet alert focus that allows full awareness of your state as you fall asleep. As you lie in bed, focus on your intention to remain aware of your state of consciousness, and notice when you begin dreaming.

Choose an aspect of your present experience to which you can anchor your attention as you relax into sleep. Your physical senses are a useful reference point; try scanning parts of your body or observing your breath. Keeping your attention on your body has sleep-inducing qualities and can help you be vigilant of sleep paralysis and other bodily sensations that can signal nearness to dreaming.

With a detached, present-focused awareness, you can also observe the visual images that arise as you fall deeper into sleep—allow them to change on their own as they develop into immersive dream scenes.

As you remain focused on your present state, notice if you start experiencing abstract, dreamlike thoughts without getting caught up in them. If you get swept away by these thoughts, you'll lose focus and drift into a nonlucid dream. Instead, anchor your attention back onto your intention to remember your current state of consciousness.

Visualization

Rather than passively observing your experience of falling asleep, you can aid the transition by using active visualization. In particular, visualizing movements is a powerful WILD induction technique.

During LaBerge's experiments on prolonging lucid dreaming, several participants reported that they were able to reenter a lucid dream after waking by imagining themselves repeatedly performing a specific movement—spinning their body or rubbing their hands together. Visualizing other types of repetitive motion can also help, like imagining yourself rocking back and forth as if in a rocking chair, swinging side to side as if in a hammock, swimming, walking, pedaling a bicycle, or writing "I am dreaming" on a chalkboard. Soon these movements may begin to feel real, leading you into a lucid dream during which you continue the repetitive action with your dream body instead of your imagination.

If you're lying on your back, you're more likely to experience awareness during sleep paralysis. If you're a deep sleeper who has difficulty being aware during wake-sleep transitions, try elevating your sleeping position with propped pillows. This may lighten your sleep and help you pay better attention to your experience.

ADVENTURES IN LUCIDITY

To induce WILD, I interrupted my sleep for 30 minutes. When I returned to bed, I focused on imagining that I was writing "This is a dream" over and over on a piece of paper. Soon I could feel the friction of the pen gliding across the paper, and in a flash, I clearly saw the paper and ink.

Excited now, I knew I was close to entering the lucid dream. I suddenly felt the pull of sleep paralysis—my body heavy and buzzing in bed with a vivid energy. I knew that I was dreaming, yet I couldn't move my dream body. I decided to imagine myself rocking back and forth. The imagined movements swiftly became real, and my dream body was rocking back and forth in bed. With as much force as I could muster, I finally thrust myself out of bed to find myself in a small airplane flying over a scenic countryside. I had always wanted to skydive in a lucid dream and realized this was my chance.

I jumped from the plane without a parachute, arching my back and somersaulting as I gleefully fell through the air. I repeated "This is a dream" to help myself stay lucid as long as possible. I effortlessly switched from falling to flying as I gently guided myself onto the ground.

Remember to Remember

Remembering is the cornerstone of inducing lucid dreaming. First, remember your dreams so you have a sense of what to focus your waking mind's intentions on for becoming lucid. Secondly, use prospective memory strategies to help you remember to notice you are dreaming tonight. This is accomplished by reminding yourself to notice dreamsigns, which are the distinguishing characteristics of your dreams that can cue you to remember your true state of consciousness. You can increase your chances of lucid dreaming by integrating supportive practices into your induction regimen, like WILD techniques and sleep interruption. With a commitment to your practice, your application of these skills should become more effective and effortless over time.

CHAPTER 4

IN LUCID
DREAMS

nducing lucidity is only one part of the necessary skill set for productive lucid dreams. Once you're in the lucid dream, you will need additional skills to help you sustain your lucidity, prevent yourself from waking up before you want to, and steer the dream in a helpful direction. This chapter introduces skills for prolonging lucidity, achieving meaningful goals during your dreams, and working with challenging images to nurture personal growth. The possibilities for exploration in lucid dreams are endless, and we'll touch on some potentially fruitful areas.

One thing to know going in: If you continue to pursue lucid dreaming, you will inevitably encounter the darker aspects of human consciousness, including nightmares or uncomfortable images. Fortunately, there are research-supported techniques for transforming this material. Confronting the challenges you encounter during your dreams with creativity and compassion can push you toward a greater sense of wholeness, making more room for exploring higher, more transcendent states of consciousness through lucid dreaming.

Stabilizing Lucidity

Once you realize you're dreaming, it's common to react impulsively and forget your goal, which means a missed chance to explore something important to you. There's also the challenge of awakening prematurely, as well as forgetting that you're dreaming. These obstacles can be circumvented by training in the following skills.

REMEMBER YOUR GOAL

Lucid dreams are of less value if you don't make good use of your time while lucid. Beginners are prone to going along with the dream's narrative without realizing the opportunity to create a more meaningful experience. Before bed each night, have a clear and meaningful goal in mind that you'll implement should you have a lucid dream.

When practicing the MILD technique, incorporate remembering your goal into the rescripted version of your dream, and rehearse achieving it.

POSTPONE AWAKENINGS

One of the most common stumbling blocks once you're lucid is waking up from the lucid dream too quickly.

Classic works suggest that visually focusing on dream objects may delay a premature awakening. However, this technique is problematic because the visual imagery is often the first to fade when an awakening is imminent.

Through a series of investigations, however, LaBerge identified two actions that can postpone awakenings: spinning and hand-rubbing.

When you perform an action in a dream, your brain's activity looks similar to when you perform the same action in waking life. Spinning your dream body activates your vestibular system, which is responsible for your sense of balance and orientation in space, even though your physical body isn't moving. Your vestibular system is closely linked with the brain areas that are involved in REM sleep and visual processing. This is likely why spinning can postpone awakenings—it activates your brain's REM sleep and visual systems, enhancing the dream state's stability and vividness.

In a lucid dream, as soon as you sense that you might be waking, practice spinning your dream body by standing up with your arms extended and spin your dream body as fast as you can. Focus on this type of whirling until you find yourself in a new dream scene. If you wake up, lie still and imagine that, for at least a minute, your body is still spinning as you try to fall back asleep, which could help you reenter the lucid dream.

Here's a report that provides an example of extending a lucid dream by "spinning":

I'm driving in fog, concerned that I'll have an accident, when I let go of the wheel, realizing, "This is a dream!" The car melts away and it feels amazing. I keep going into the blackness and remember that I should spin. Next, I'm in my body in bed. I imagine myself spinning, and then I find myself standing again and spinning really fast. All kinds of scenes and colors are passing before my eyes. As I spin, I keep going back and forth from my dream body to my body in bed. When I stop, I see my dear relative who has passed on in real life. I say, "See? I told you I could do this." He says, "I believe in you." We embrace and chat.

Hand-rubbing

The science of perception has shown that imagining that you perceive something with one of your five senses makes you less sensitive to perceiving something in the real world using that sense. In other words, if you're performing an action with your dream body, you're less likely to become aware of the competing sensations of your physical body lying still in bed. This means that performing certain actions in your dreams, like rubbing your hands together, could prevent your attention from shifting back to your waking-world sensations, thereby prolonging your lucid dream.

Here's an account that illustrates the use of hand-rubbing when the visual imagery of the dream is fading:

I realize I'm dreaming. The dream becomes dark and it feels like I'm about to wake up, so I start rubbing my hands together. The details of the dream scene gradually become more vivid. I see a Middle Eastern city and blue sky over sea. I begin to fly over the streets, feeling exhilarated as I swoop down to touch the trees.

So as soon as you sense you're waking up, vigorously rub your dream hands together. Keep your full attention on your senses and feel the friction and heat between your hands. If you wake up, try to fall back asleep while imagining the sensation of hand-rubbing for at least a minute to help you induce a WILD.

Be calm

Many lucid dreamers believe that the initial excitement from becoming lucid sometimes wakes them up. While it's possible to explore powerful emotions in dreams without waking, stronger emotions are indeed known to activate the brain and body, which could hasten waking up. If you get too excited after becoming lucid, step back from the emotion and calmly refocus your mind on your lucid dreaming goal.

DON'T FORGET THAT YOU'RE DREAMING

It is easy to quickly forget that you're dreaming and lose lucidity so that you become reabsorbed into the nonlucid dream state. To prevent yourself from forgetting you are dreaming, you'll need to learn how to balance remembering that you're dreaming while actively participating in the dream.

Repeat "This is a dream." Continuously remind yourself to remain lucid. Try repeating the phrase "This is a dream" to yourself every few seconds. If you're trying to achieve goals or attempting to explore a narrative in your lucid dream, frequently reanchor your attention on the fact that you're dreaming. The pull of nonlucidity can be even stronger in certain situations, like when you encounter strong emotions or mesmerizing beauty. When you have these encounters, step back from your experience to remind yourself that you're dreaming.

Recognize false awakenings. The dream state is constructed from our mental models of reality. Once you know you're dreaming, your mind expects that you'll wake up soon. These expectations frequently lead to a dream scene in which you have awoken in your bed. These false awakenings can include convincing replicas of your bedroom, compromising your ability to stay lucid. Given the frequency of false awakenings, you should learn to suspect, when you wake up from lucid dreams, that you're still dreaming. Conduct a rereading state test (see page 57) to figure out whether you're actually awake.

PRACTICE POINT: RESCRIPT LUCID DREAMS

Even if a lucid dream didn't turn out the way you'd hoped, you can use it as an opportunity to better plan out what you'll do the next time you become lucid. In the practice point below, the three Rs technique is modified to help you refine your lucid dreaming skills and prepare your mind for the next time you're lucid.

For example, if you forgot to spin your dream body when the imagery began to fade, mentally rescript and rehearse the dream as if you did remember to spin, and remind yourself to spin next time you're in a similar situation. Or let's say you wanted to explore a pre-intended goal but impulsively began flying and missed your opportunity. Then you can rescript the dream as though you did remember to implement your goal. Repeat these steps as many times as necessary in order to feel that your intention to respond differently in future lucid dreams is firmly set.

1. **Rescript.** Using a recent lucid dream, choose a point at which you'll envision yourself back in the dream. But this time, rescript the dream so that you respond in a way that results in a more favorable outcome.

2. **Rehearse.** Mentally rehearse the rescripted version of your dream. Imagine the new version as many times as needed to clearly visualize yourself experiencing the rescripted version of your lucid dream.

3. **Remind.** Remind yourself that next time you encounter a similar challenge, you will respond in the way you intend. For example, you might say, "Next time I become lucid, I will remember my goal to _____." Or, "Next time the imagery in a dream begins to fade, I will remember to spin my dream body."

Endless Possibilities

In the absence of physical and social constraints, the lucid dream state offers innovative ways to explore your mind and to practice bending reality to your will. Let's explore the possibilities to spark your imagination about how you might like to use lucidity in your own dreams.

EXERCISE CONTROL

Lucid dreams are the perfect playground for learning about your mind's malleable nature and how to intentionally experience realities of value. There certainly are degrees of control that you can experience in a lucid dream, but even if you are good at controlling what happens in your dreams, your lucid dreams may not always go as you intend.

Start by changing what you have the most control over: your own thoughts, expectations, and behavior. Instead of automatically reacting to your experiences, step back and broaden your awareness toward the full range of possibilities. Deconstruct any limiting beliefs and reframe your experiences to help you achieve your goals.

One of the most remarkable things about lucid dreaming is its capacity to demonstrate how your own mental models of the world manifest in dream content. Your wishes, belief systems, expectations, attitudes, and interpretations in lucid dreams can have a direct and immediate effect on your dreamed experience. By learning to change your mind, you can change your reality.

Practice changing your dreams for the sheer sake of it. Experiment with the lack of stability and permanence of dreamed objects. Walk through walls, make items vanish, or manipulate objects' size, quantity, form, or speed. Travel to a different point in time. Experiment with changing your locus of perception: Be in more than one body at a time, enter someone else's body, or shape-shift into an animal.

Draw from the power of expectation and visualization to prompt your intended changes. Ask the dream to help you experience what you desire; your dream characters may even be willing to help you create intended scenarios if you make a polite request.

When you declare your intentions, sometimes your dream will respond to your request in a different way than you expect, so keep an open mind. At other times, acceptance of reality—not control—may be what is most needed for a better outcome.

INCREASE POSITIVE EMOTIONS

Knowing that you're unrestricted by your waking life's typical rules lets you have more adventure and fun. Use your lucidity to marvel at the wonders of your mind, and wake up feeling amazing and ready to take on the day. Visit exciting new places. Do things you normally wouldn't. Fly through waterfall-lined valleys. Sail through the South Pacific's crystal waters. Meditate in a sacred temple. Converse with an animal. Meet a favorite celebrity, artist, or an admired person in history. See your favorite musician in concert and ask for a personal serenade. Explore your hobbies and interests through the lens of lucidity. Surf big waves. Drive race cars. Dance with fire. Swim with a pod of orcas. Try rooftop parkour over a stunning urban landscape. Role-play in your favorite fantasy, superhero, or sci-fi story line. Basically, do anything that would bring a giant grin to your face.

DREAM SEX

Free from the constraints of ordinary reality, lucid dreams provide a safe space to explore your sexuality with more depth and breadth than you might be able to in waking life. Sometimes sex is thought of as a lower-order activity of lucid dreaming. Though any lucid dream activity can be done in excess, this attitude disregards the benefits of lucid dream sex to health, happiness, and the potential to connect with sexuality's sacred dimensions. Dream sex can also be a way to learn how to navigate lucid dreams more skillfully, express yourself more authentically, and stretch your identity as a sexual being. Exploring pleasure and wish fulfillment, in whatever form it arises, can play an important role in nurturing your growth as a lucid dreamer.

SKILL REHEARSAL

Humans have evolved "imaging" abilities, including imagination and dreaming, to rehearse responses to situations in ways that help them thrive. Lucid dreaming has unique advantages over rehearsing skills in your imagination, nonlucid dreams, or the waking world; the state's inherent safety and creativity, its evocative realism, and its accessibility to preferred and meaningful experiences can make lucid dreams an ideal practice field for testing new ways of relating with reality.

Say, for example, you want to improve your three-point shot in basketball. The best way to improve, of course, is to practice in waking reality. But perhaps your lucid dreams can give you extra practice when you can't get to the basketball court, or when your physical body needs rest and recovery. You can get personalized feedback on your form, as well as inspirational motivation, from your favorite pro player. You can discover more about how your mental state impacts your throw accuracy when external factors, like physical or social limitations, don't hold power over your reality.

Consider an everyday skill, sport, or art form that you'd like to explore improving in your lucid dreams. Since the best way to improve skills is to practice while awake, consider how practicing during the lucid dream state can give you an edge when you select your goal.

CREATIVE PROBLEM-SOLVING

You can transform your dreams into your own personal incubator for fresh insights, inspiration, and ingenuity. Consider a problem you're dealing with in your daily life. It could be an issue at work, or something related to relationships, emotions, health, finances, or greater society. Once lucid, seek out a dream to help you explore this issue. For example:

I decided to use my lucid dreams to discover how to finish an art piece that I was struggling to complete. I expected that the dreamed version would look the same as the real artwork, but this was a mistake. As I took the piece out of my closet, I was pierced by a beautiful, blazing, fiery blue color that was alive and moving. A swarm of mermaids were swimming, swirling, and dancing around the artwork. Their tails shimmered like kaleidoscopes, and the background was checkered with shifting sections of intricate geometric patterns. It was incredible! When I woke up, I finished the painting by integrating the mermaids, and once done, the painting took on a whole other level of personal meaning.

You can quickly spin your dream body to produce scene transitions that are ideal for exploring your goals. As you spin, the visual imagery of the current dream scene will blur until you stop and find yourself in another scene. You might find that you can spin to a preferred dream scene just by intending it. The next time you're lucid and want to change scenes to explore a goal, try these steps:

1. Out loud, declare your intention to transport to a specific dream scene, or request that your dreaming mind create it for you.

2. Stand up with your arms out and spin your dream body as fast as you can, for 10 to 20 seconds.

3. As you spin, expect and intend for the new scene to allow you to explore your goal. Visualize what the new scene might look like. Repeat, "The next dream scene will be _____," filling in the blank with your desired destination.

Transforming Your Nightmares

Unresolved psychological conflicts tend to be symbolically represented in dreams. When dream content threatens your sense of safety or security, dreams turn into nightmares, which range from mildly distressing to terrifying. Mild distress may include the experience of things going wrong, being unable to find something, or anxiety about a social interaction. More distressing nightmares may result in waking with intense negative emotions and are sometimes experienced as repetitive, disturbing, or out of control.

Lucid dreaming's creative problem-solving potential presents a unique opportunity to renegotiate nightmare situations. The increased sense of safety and freedom from normal rules is ideal for transforming their outcomes.

APPROACHES TO NIGHTMARES

All humans are wired to seek happiness and avoid pain and discomfort. Problems arise when our automatic responses to challenges keep us stuck in a loop of running away from our fears, fighting with ourselves or others, or not doing enough to resolve an issue. This cycling between flight, fight, or freeze responses has long been ingrained in our evolutionary history to help us adapt and survive.

But there's a more effective approach for supporting your personal growth. This is known as *self-integration*, in which you

Table 4.1: Responses to Nightmares—Pros and Cons

RESPONSE	DESCRIPTION
Avoid	You steer clear or try to escape something in a dream. You might wake yourself up, run and hide, fly away, or make the image disappear. You may avoid engaging by choosing to do something else. You may be dismissive, disregarding your dream content as though it's not important or relevant to you.

show a willingness to engage with the uncomfortable or distress-ing parts of reality in a way that reflects a deeper connection with yourself.

People tend to respond to stressful dreams using one of the four strategies described in the table on pages 84–87. Each approach comes with its own set of advantages and disadvantages, which vary in importance depending on the nature of the night-mare and your individual context. But overall, a self-integration approach foreshadows the best outcome to resolving nightmares. As self-integration is a personal growth concept that extends beyond just nightmares, the next section of this book elaborates on exploring it in lucid dreams.

Read through the table and consider the pros and cons when forming your own responses in lucid dreams, and also when you practice rescripting your dreams after you wake up.

PROS	CONS
You get immediate stress relief. If you don't yet have the skills to respond adaptively to stressful dreams, avoidance may be preferable. A temporary distancing from nightmare imagery can also give you a clearer perspective about how to respond better in the future.	Avoidance is a short-term solution that ends up reinforcing your fears and making it likely that the stress will return in some form.

RESPONSE	DESCRIPTION
Confront and Conquer	You fight back or try to defend yourself. You may initiate or escalate aggression or try to manipulate or win. You might express anger, defiance, or "speak your truth."
Go with the Flow	You do nothing or keep doing what you were already doing. You might be submissive, passive, or take a "wait and see" approach until you wake up. You may just respond the same way that you usually would, or how you have responded to similar challenges in the past.
Seek Self-Integration	Self-integration is an ever-evolving process of becoming more whole and complete as a person. You recognize that all parts of the dream represent something within yourself that is in conflict, or a part of yourself that you reject, fear, or do not accept. Then you attempt to reconcile or make peace with these unaccepted parts of yourself.

PROS	CONS
A strongly assertive approach may be what is needed for personal growth in certain situations, leading to a feeling of triumph, confidence, empowerment, or feeling heard and respected.	Tholey's research found that this approach tends to backfire. The more aggressive you are with hostile dream figures, the angrier, stronger, more violent, or frightening these figures will become.
There may be advantages to surrendering control in lucid dreams. In some cases, your attempts to overly control outcomes may be what is causing distress in the first place.	You could miss opportunities to transform your reality. Tholey found that defenseless behavior almost always led to more fear or discouragement, and an increase in the size and power of hostile dream figures.
The self-integration approach can stop nightmares from recurring and promote personal growth. Tholey showed that it reduces how threatening hostile figures appear, and sometimes reveals the meaning of the dream more clearly. For example, a dark figure that is chasing you may transform, when confronted, into a person with whom you have conflict in waking life.	You may not be ready to integrate what the imagery symbolizes into your self-concept, or you may not have the skills to do this effectively yet.

PRACTICE POINT: RESCRIPT A NIGHTMARE

Rescripting the story line of your nightmares so that they include lucidity is a rich practice that can enhance self-understanding and prepare you to respond to stress in future lucid dreams with more resilience.

In keeping with the **three Rs** of your MILD practice, **rescript** nightmares as though you had become lucid and facilitated a better outcome. Write the rescripted version in your dream journal, if you wish. **Rehearse** new outcomes in your imagination and **remind** yourself to become lucid the next time you're having a nightmare. It is useful to do this right when you wake up from nightmares, but it may be easier to do in the daytime when you've had more distance from the dream.

After rescripting your dream, decide what type of response (avoid, confront and conquer, go with the flow, or seek self-integration) you used in the revised version of your dream. No matter what category seems to fit best, remember that these categories are not necessarily mutually exclusive. In fact, all lucid dream behavior may reflect progress on the path toward self-integration at least on some level, though some responses certainly demonstrate this better than others.

ADVENTURES IN LUCIDITY

I was having a series of WILDs during which I would get stuck in sleep paralysis and be visited by figures such as a corpse, a mangled woman, and a mummy under my bed. I learned that these images were representations of my own self—parts of me that had been wounded, lost, or were suffering. At the time, I didn't know how to accept this, but I vowed that during my next lucid nightmare, I would overcome my fear and engage these figures.

As expected, I was frozen again in sleep paralysis the next time I was lucid, but this time, a monstrous creature was heaving with anger at my bedside. Though the paralysis would not let me speak to the figure, I knew I did not need a voice. Instead, I projected my thoughts telepathically to communicate. I introduced myself and said that I was sorry that it was angry or sad, and that I was there if it wanted to talk.

To my surprise and delight, it began to wag its tail. I became unstuck and began to pet it. I gave the being a hug, and it disappeared into my arms. After that, the nightmares stopped recurring.

Self-Integration

Self-integration is a concept that has been described throughout human history. It's about creating connection and harmony between all parts of oneself. A helpful outlook in the lucid dream state is to view your dream imagery as representing something about yourself or your life. By interacting with these images, you can learn how to defragment your identity and embrace all aspects of who you are, including your unrecognized strengths, as well as the parts that you dislike or disown. This process of integrating your personality can help you reduce inner conflicts and improve your relationship with yourself and others. It can also help you dissolve the illusion of separateness between what you deem to be "you" and "not you," which is necessary to move beyond the self—to experience self-transcendence and spiritual awakening.

DREAM ARCHETYPES AND THE "SHADOW"

An archetype is a universal symbol that is seen in lore across cultures, religions, and history. Today, we commonly see archetypes dramatized as characters in books and movies, such as the wounded healer, the villain, or the jokester. In your dreams, archetypes are not just the characters, but also the objects, settings, story lines, and other elements. Examples of classic archetypes in dreams might include an apocalyptic flood, the first day of school, your inner hero, or a mother and child.

The *shadow* is an important archetype that represents the parts of you or your life that you have not fully accepted. Often, the shadow signifies something that you are in conflict with, reject, or do not identify with. This could represent a part of your personality, a relationship, a past memory, a part of you that is suffering, or something related to broader society. The shadow can also be a neutral or even positive part of yourself that's not fully developed.

Carl Jung believed that contemplating archetypes and finding adaptive ways of relating to these images can foster self-integration. However, you don't need to understand what these images specifically mean about you to change your relationship with them.

REAL-TIME DREAM INTERPRETATION

Interpreting your dreams while you're still dreaming can add new depth to your lucid dream practice. Instead of waiting until you're awake to figure out what your dream means, adopt the view that while still dreaming, the images you're encountering are symbolic representations of parts of yourself. This will let you interact with your dreams with a greater degree of intimacy and intellect. You can directly ask your dream figures what they symbolize, and request recurring dreams to reveal their meaning. Lucidity applied in this way readily mirrors you back to yourself with more clarity. Here's an example of fostering self-integration by understanding your dream's meaning while lucid dreaming.

Panicked that I wasn't prepared to take a math test, I remembered that I graduated long ago and that this must be a dreamsign. I thought, "Math problems? What could that mean?" The teacher seemed to be the most qualified to respond. I stood up and asked, "What kinds of problems am I trying to solve in my waking life?" At that moment, she turned into my wife and told me that I've been ignoring our relationship too much. I apologized and said that I know our problems are complex, but I would try to work on them more. She thanked me, and I awoke feeling like a weight had been lifted.

CONCILIATORY DIALOGUES

One of the most constructive ways to engage unintegrated parts of the self, such as hostile dream characters, is through conciliatory dialogues. Lucid dreams can respond to this change in attitude toward the shadow with a gentle interplay that promotes healing and personal growth. Here are suggestions to help you organize your interactions with threatening or shadow-like figures while lucid dreaming.

Remember that you are safe. Shadow figures are not of any physical threat to you in lucid dreams. Try to see them in another light; for instance, as a part of yourself that is suffering or needs help.

Be friendly, open, and curious. Smile, look your dream characters in the eye, and use nonthreatening body language and gestures. Show that you are willing to connect.

Ask questions. Seek to understand the figure or your situation. Ask shadow figures to tell you about themselves. A shared understanding can help you resolve the psychological conflict that these figures represent.

Practice compassion. Tell shadow figures how you empathize with their feelings. Express warm wishes that they may be free from their suffering.

Offer and ask for help. Ask, "How can I help you?" or, "Can you help me?" If you have a specific idea of something that could help, propose it to the figure in your dream.

Exchange gifts. Offer gratitude and a gift to the figure, perhaps by pulling one out of your pocket. Ask the figure if it has a gift for you.

Occasionally, you might find that shadow figures in lucid dreams are uncooperative with even your most wholehearted attempts to reconcile with them. If necessary, set boundaries with the figure or stand up for yourself, which might produce a better outcome for you than feeling helpless.

HEALING DREAMS

Since ancient times, people have integrated mental imagery into cultural practices for healing, which has included the use of dreams. Your dreams are a landscape that dramatizes your memories, difficult emotions, wounds, and unfinished business—you can use lucid dreaming to intentionally explore all of these to ease your suffering and nurture self-integration. Dreams also contain wisdom about the body, including illnesses, providing ways to heal the mind-body connection through lucid dreaming.

They say that time heals all wounds, but a year had passed since my mother died and I was still struggling. In my dreams, she looked just like she did while alive, but sad. These dreams always had some sort of tension between us, and I would awaken grief-stricken. I began learning how to lucid dream so that I could see her more often. I'd repeat before bed, "When I see my mom tonight, I will remember that I'm dreaming." When I saw my mom days later, it clicked. I said, "Mom! This is a dream! Let's dance!" I took her in my arms and twirled her around. Her favorite song began playing out of nowhere. We talked for quite some time. I was so happy that I was able to experience her again. I realized that my relationship with her was not totally lost. I still look forward to her visits whenever I go to sleep.

ADVENTURES IN LUCIDITY

I became lucid during a dream in which I was traveling in Europe with my fiancé. I grabbed his hand and we began soaring over a plaza with Romanesque fountains. I remarked that we should try to heal the stubborn patch of dermatitis on his knee, which he had had for months. I placed my hand over it, and recited a popular Buddhist mantra: Om mani padme hum.

When I woke up, I told him about the dream, but the rash on his leg looked the same. The next day, he noticed that the top layer of skin seemed to change form. I joked that it was probably from the "lucid dreaming medicine" I had given him.

A few days later, we were vacationing in Hawaii. Hiking behind him on a steep, wet trail, I pointed out that his skin was looking better. I suggested that we honor the dream with a ritual, so I rubbed his knee while repeating the mantra again. A week later, his skin was completely healed.

Maybe the homeopathic medicines he had been taking for several months finally started to work the day after my lucid dream, but it was hard to dismiss the coincidental timing. Perhaps there's more to healing oneself—and others—through lucid dreaming than people realize.

Spiritual Awakening

At the heart of lucid dreaming is its capacity for spiritual connection and exploring existential matters. Unobscured by the material world's sensory experiences, you can more freely explore the boundlessness of your mind when lucid. The benefits of a spiritual focus during lucid dreams may include experiencing a stronger sense of love, compassion, beauty, and interconnectedness in your everyday life. You may find that lucid dreaming helps you let go of attachments and parts of your identity that aren't serving you well. Many lucid dreamers report that sublime states are more readily accessible from the lucid dream state.

As you might guess, there's not a simple formula for having a spiritually transcendent lucid dream. It can help, of course, to set intentions that are aligned with your own spiritual beliefs and practices. For instance, you might engage in meditation or prayer or interact with a spiritual teacher, ancestor, guide, or animal in your lucid dreams. You could ask an existential question in the dream or ask to be shown a metaphor that helps you understand the source of all being.

> "Transcendental experiences are advantageous in that they help us detach from fixed ideas about ourselves. The less we identify with who we think we are, the more likely we are to one day discover who we really are."
>
> —STEPHEN LaBERGE, PhD

I became lucid in a dark dream scene with two figures flailing and waving, as if desperately trying to get my attention. When I noticed them, they pointed upward to a hole in the blackness—a window to a big blue sky. As a bodiless point of awareness, I floated up to it and found that the darkness was actually an endless black wall that spanned in all directions. I looked through the window and saw a bright circle of white light pressed against the wall below, as though it was hiding. I recognized this light from previous lucid dreams, and with that, it began to expand and envelop me. All sense of "me" dissipated into ecstasy. There was no sense of separation, no "I" and no "it." Everything was one. There are no words to describe it.

OUT-OF-BODY EXPERIENCES

The topic of out-of-body experiences (OBEs) comes up often for people who are exploring the world of lucid dreaming. Let's be clear: Lucid dreaming is not the same as an OBE. However, these two anomalous frontiers of consciousness do share some over-lapping features, and, very likely, similar brain processes.

An OBE is the perception that you're experiencing your focal point of awareness from outside of your physical body. Using the most rigorous sense of this definition, all dreams might be viewed as a type of OBE because your perspective takes place not from the view of your physical body, but from your dream body. But dreams—both nonlucid and lucid—can also contain experiences in which your locus of perception is different from usual. You might notice that you're a bodiless point of awareness in space, or that you see a twin of yourself in another location.

Reports of voluntarily induced OBEs—called *astral projection* in the occult literature—tend to share strikingly similar features with sleep paralysis and WILDs: As you lie down to rest, you interpret unusual sensations as though you're separating from your physical body. Vibrations, floating over the bed, rolling onto the floor, or other bizarre sensory experiences can occur.

One study by LaBerge confirmed that people who reported OBEs had these experiences while dreaming. In most cases, the key difference between WILDs and OBEs that are induced while resting in bed is the interpretation of the experience. If you believe that you are having an OBE, you interpret that you're actually outside your physical body exploring the physical universe, the dream, or some other plane of existence. In a WILD, you interpret that you are asleep and perceiving the lucid dream state.

OBEs can be induced in other ways: with certain drugs, during advanced meditation, and under extreme physical and mental stress, as in, near-death experiences. The Dalai Lama, among others, has described advanced practices for transferring consciousness out of the body, which may involve visiting real places in the universe or other planes of existence. In short, a subset of OBEs and WILDs may share similar features and brain processes, but lucid dreaming can't account for all cases of OBEs.

The spectrum of conscious experience is vast and not limited to the narrow mental models with which we usually perceive the world. Indeed, non-ordinary states like OBEs and lucid dreaming have much to teach us about the infinite nature of the mind, the processes of dying and separating from physical reality, and humanity's biggest mysteries.

Practice, Practice, Practice

While this chapter presented a starting point for stabilizing and exploring lucid dreams, there is much more to explore. Be creative, patient, and methodical in your approaches to support your growth and the ability to achieve your goals. Even if a lucid dream doesn't go the way you wanted, remember that you can still learn from the experience, which is valuable in and of itself.

Sometimes your attempts to direct or stabilize the lucid dream will work; other times they may fall short. The more trial-and-error experiences you have in lucid dreams, the more you will learn to maneuver in this state with skill and grace.

Don't give up, and remember to stay open to the dream's natural wisdom without attempting to overly control it. It's possible that your lucid dreams will hand you one of your wishes on a silver platter when you least expect it, or you may just find that what you truly desire was different from what you originally thought. In the next chapter, you'll get directions on how to take your practice even further.

CHAPTER 5

GROWING YOUR PRACTICE

No matter where you are in your development as a lucid dreamer, there's always more to learn—one of the things you can grow to truly appreciate about lucid dreaming is how, indeed, you'll be constantly learning.

There are many directions you can take to grow your practice of lucid dreaming. One of the main challenges for beginners is inducing the lucid state with enough frequency to learn from their experiences. This is where a practical tool called "the nightly experience log" comes in to help you refine your awareness and memory of what you're experiencing over the course of the night.

This chapter also offers daytime skills to complement and expand your practice. People who meditate, for example, are known to have better lucid dreaming abilities. By being more observant of the present moment and of the contents of your own mind, you'll be more prepared to recognize when your present reality is actually a dream. For that reason, this chapter also covers mindfulness meditation, which is essentially a form of attention training that helps you be less distractible and more in tune with what's happening in the here and now.

As explained earlier in this book, developing a heightened focus on remembering your dreams can magnify the interweaving themes from your sleeping and waking worlds. To that end, you might be interested in extending your lucid dreaming skills to enhance your waking life. One magnificent thing that you learn as your practice deepens is that the world model your brain constructs while awake can be just as malleable as when you're lucid dreaming. So we will also explore the concept of "waking lucidity," which applies the qualities of lucid dream consciousness, such as a heightened sense of clarity, purpose, and creativity, to nurturing your waking condition.

On occasion, beginners express misconceptions and worries about lucid dreaming—I will discuss these to alleviate any undue concerns so they don't become obstacles in your growth. I also cover a few of the common mistakes novice lucid dreamers tend to make so your efforts to lucid dream can be as efficient as possible.

The Nightly Experience Log

To take your induction skills further, you'll need to continue refining your attention to your nightly experiences. Most people have very little awareness about what happens over the course of a night's sleep. We lie down, close our eyes, and often the next thing we know, it's morning. This "gap" in consciousness is often called being "unconscious." But just because you don't remember them doesn't mean that you weren't having all sorts of conscious experiences.

The nightly experience log is designed to help you focus on becoming more conscious of what you experience during the night (see table 5.1 on page 104). As you know, everyone experiences brief awakenings several times per night, whether they're remembered or not. Completing this log can help you set your mind to explicitly notice these awakenings so you can remember to apply induction and dream-recall skills.

Each time you wake up during the night, you'll fill out an event row of the log to record the time, the type of experience you just had (WILD, DILD, nonlucid dreaming, thinking, etc.), and rate how well you recall the experience.

Motivated beginners typically find this log easy to complete, and that it enhances their nocturnal awareness. An added benefit of keeping a nightly experience log is that it can increase wakefulness during the night, which promotes lucidity when you return to sleep.

MATERIALS

Keep a few things within arm's reach of your bed: a printed copy of the log (see page 104), a writing surface, a pen, a digital clock, and a light. If you don't have a copier, use a blank page in your dream journal to code your nightly experiences.

MEMORIZE THE KEY

Before you can rate your nightly experiences, you'll need to familiarize yourself with tables 5.2 and 5.3 (see pages 105–109). At first, it may help to keep the key next to your bed so you can reference the code anchors during awakenings. But with a little time and practice, most people easily memorize the codes.

AT LIGHTS-OUT

Write down the date and time you turned out the lights to go to sleep. Before falling asleep, resolve to wake up from your dreams and remember them. Apply the three Rs: Practice rescripting and rehearsing recent dreams as if they were lucid. Remind yourself to remember that you are dreaming when you are dreaming. Fall asleep.

DURING AWAKENINGS

Each time you awaken, fill out an event row of the nightly experience log. Write down the time, code the type of experience you were having, and rate how well you remember it. Carefully considering the types of dreams you have and how well you remember them can help you become more aware of experiences that will help you understand what it actually takes to lucid dream. If you remember a dream, you don't have to write the details in your journal, but you can if you want. You can complete up to seven rows of the log, but if you have fewer than seven awakenings over the night, leave the rest blank.

Table 5.1: Nightly Experience Log*

DATE			
LIGHTS-OUT			
EVENT	TIME	EXPERIENCE	RECALL
1			
2			
3			
4			
5			
6			
7			
RISE TIME			
COMMENTS:			

*Adapted from LaBerge, Stephen, and Kristen LaMarca, 2015 -2018. Nightly Experience Type Recall and Time (NETRAT) Log. Unpublished.

Table 5.2: Experience Types

EXPERIENCE CODE	DESCRIPTION	EXAMPLE
/	**Nothing**. You remember nothing before the moment you woke up, and you don't even have the feeling that you were just dreaming.	*"I woke up and had no sense that my mind was just active. I don't remember anything."*
F	**Forgot**. You have the impression that you were dreaming something but immediately and completely forgot all contents of the dream.	*"I was just dreaming something, but as I went to write it down, I couldn't remember anything. I don't even have a sense of the mood from the dream."*
T	**Thinking**. You were thinking about something but weren't embedded within a visually driven scene with a narrative sequence of events.	*"I was having thoughts about the project I'm working on. It was like I was trying to figure something out."*

EXPERIENCE CODE	DESCRIPTION	EXAMPLE
N	**Nonlucid dream.** You were dreaming but didn't explicitly think about how you were dreaming.	*"I've been trying for a long time to find a department at work, except it's also my high school and an airport. I pass the front office staff, who solicit me to take my school picture; I decline."*
S	**Sublucid dream.** You wondered whether you were dreaming but concluded that you were awake or did not become lucid.	*"I'm scurrying down the hall late for class when I notice that this is just like my recurring dreams about college. I briefly think, 'Wouldn't it be great if this were a dream?' Then I try to slip into the back of the classroom without the professor noticing my tardiness."*

EXPERIENCE CODE	DESCRIPTION	EXAMPLE
D	**Dream-Initiated Lucid Dream (DILD).** A dream in which you realized you were dreaming amid an ongoing dream, perhaps by noticing an anomaly.	*"I'm distressed from trying to take care of my baby, who will not stop crying. I then realize that this baby cannot be mine because my children are all grown. I'm shocked to realize that I have been dreaming this whole scenario. The baby suddenly disappears from my arms."*

EXPERIENCE CODE	DESCRIPTION	EXAMPLE
W	**Wake-Initiated Lucid Dream (WILD).** A dream in which you retained consciousness (lucidity) from the waking state as the dream began. You knew you were dreaming as soon as you started to dream.	*"I'm watching hypnagogic images of human figures forming in the dark. I see a woman's legs walking around and I imagine myself taking steps in sync with hers. As I imagine my feet stepping right and left, the movements suddenly begin to feel real. I swiftly transfer into a full dream scene, now admiring a classic European town square. It's gorgeous."*
O	**Other Event.** Use this code if your experience was something else, or if you want to note that you got out of bed for an hour, for example. Add an explanation in the comments section.	*"I got out of bed for 30 minutes to read, then tried to induce a WILD when I went back to sleep."*

Table 5.3: Degree of Dream Recall

RECALL RATING	DESCRIPTION
0	NOT AT ALL, OR NIL. No specific content, not even the feeling that you were dreaming. Nothing, plain and simple. Unlike the next level.
0.1	FORGOT. You have the impression that you were dreaming something, but you immediately forgot all of the dream's content.
1	MINIMUM SPECIFIC CONTENT. The least nonzero amount; almost none, just a fragment. Perhaps some vague but lingering image, thought, or feeling.
2	GIST OF AT LEAST ONE SCENE. You know you were in some situation, and something happened.
3	MODERATE AMOUNT. You remember major events, sequences, emotions, and thoughts.
4	ALMOST ALL. You have a very detailed recollection of the dream, but there are some details that you are not sure of.
5	MAXIMUM RECALL. You remember all of your dream; you have a vivid recollection of it, with more details than you might describe in a dream report.

Table 5.4: Example of a Completed Nightly Experience Log

DATE	April 3		
LIGHTS-OUT	10:30 p.m.		
EVENT	**TIME**	**EXPERIENCE**	**RECALL**
1	12:04 a.m.	N	2
2	4:10 a.m.	/	0
3	4:11 a.m.	O	
4	5:20 a.m.	D	4
5	6:55 a.m.	T	0.1
6			
7			
RISE TIME	6:56 a.m.		

COMMENTS:
O = I got out of bed and stayed awake for 30 minutes. Then I practiced MILD until I fell back asleep.

As you lie back down to go to sleep, apply the three Rs of MILD to firmly set your intention to remember that you are dreaming in your next dream. Also, remind yourself to notice the next time you wake up so you can remember dreams and complete another event row of the log. Fall back asleep.

AT RISE TIME

When you're finished sleeping for the night, fill out your last event row. Apply the three Rs of MILD once more. Under "Rise Time," write down what time you got out of bed to start your day.

PRACTICE POINT: COMPLETE A NIGHTLY EXPERIENCE LOG FOR SEVEN NIGHTS

For at least seven nights (they don't need to be consecutive), fill out a nightly experience log. You can do more if you like, but seven nights should be enough to give you a good idea of what it takes to notice awakenings and pay more attention to what you remember of your sleep experiences. (For an example of what a completed log looks like, see page 110.)

Familiarize yourself with the key (see tables 5.2 and 5.3 on pages 105 and 109) and keep a printed copy of the log template (see page 104) beside your bed. Write down the time you turned out the lights to go to sleep. Resolve to recognize when you're dreaming, as well as to wake up from dreams to recall them. Then fall asleep. Whenever you notice yourself wake up, complete an event row of the log—whether you remember a dream or not. Practice another cycle of MILD, then go back to sleep. Complete more event rows of the log during subsequent awakenings. When you're finished sleeping for the night, complete your last event row and write down the time at which you got out of bed to start your day.

DREAM INCUBATION

We tend to dream about whatever is on our minds right before sleep. Some people believe that by setting the intention to have a desired dream before sleep, you'll increase the chances that you'll actually have that dream. This is called *dream incubation*, which has been practiced since ancient times for problem-solving, healing, and spiritual endeavors.

Incubating a dream means that you set an intention to dream about a specific problem or topic right before falling asleep. For example, if you're contemplating what to name your child, at bedtime, you could focus on the intention to have a dream that tells you your child's future name.

Evidence for the ability to dream about what you want is less strong for dream incubation techniques compared to lucid dreaming. This is understandable; if you're not lucid in the dream, you have less choice regarding what you'll dream about. But if you realize you are dreaming, you can remember to prompt your desired experience. Referring to the above example, you can seek out your future child in a lucid dream, perhaps by spinning your dream body while visualizing that, when you stop, your child will be present. Then you can ask, "What would you like to be named?"

You may find that you intend to become lucid so you can explore a desired topic, but even if you don't succeed at realizing you're dreaming, you can still succeed at dreaming about that topic. That is to say, you might still find the insights or experiences you were looking for in your dreams even if you didn't achieve lucidity. Being open to the wisdom of all your dreams, not just the lucid ones, can bolster your insight, motivation, and growth.

Embrace Mindfulness

As mentioned earlier, people who meditate tend to be better at lucid dreaming. If you start to pay close attention to your mind, you'll notice that it's rarely focused on the here and now as it is. Usually, the mind flits from thought to thought—rehashing the past, planning for the future, or judging current experiences.

But a mind that's highly distracted during the day often results in a distracted mind during dreaming. If we're always "asleep" and on autopilot in waking life, how can we expect to "wake up" and be lucid in dreams?

Mindfulness is a basic meditation practice that can help you to be aware of your current state of consciousness. To practice mindfulness, you observe reality as it is, rather than through the lens of your opinions. Many report that this increases clarity in their everyday decision-making, and enhances well-being and performance in a variety of ways.

While mindfulness is best learned by engaging in formal meditation exercises, like focusing on your breath while closing your eyes, the ultimate goal is to learn how to bring a quality of mindfulness to your daily activities.

The practice of mindfulness has distinct parallels with the practice of remembering that you are dreaming. To become lucid in a dream, after all, is to see your present reality as it truly is—a dream. Moreover, to stay lucid, you must keep your focus on remembering that your present reality is, in fact, a dream. By learning to observe your state while detaching from your assumptions, you'll be more prepared to detach from the biases that interfere with becoming lucid in your dreams.

There are many ways to learn and practice mindfulness; the end of this book provides a few resources. A good place to start?

Guided meditations that direct you toward observing and changing how you relate to your breath, to your physical senses, or to your external environment. Other forms of mindfulness teach you how to observe your *internal* environment, including your emotions, impulses, and mental contents.

> "Mindfulness means being awake. It means knowing what you are doing."
>
> **—JON KABAT-ZINN**

PRACTICE POINT: OBSERVE YOUR PRESENT STATE OF CONSCIOUSNESS

Set aside 10 to 20 minutes to practice this mindfulness exercise, and find a quiet place where you can sit and close your eyes. Follow the instructions below to guide your attention toward different aspects of your experience. Keep your mind focused on the here and now, without interpreting what you notice. Spend about two to three minutes on each bullet point. Consider recording yourself speaking these instructions, so you can listen along while you practice.

- **Sight.** Start with your eyes open and become visually aware of your surroundings. Notice objects, shapes, colors, patterns, and other details with a neutral, factual attitude. If you start thinking about the past or future, simply notice that your mind has strayed and anchor your attention back to your visual senses.
- **Sound.** If it feels comfortable, close your eyes. Tune into your sense of sound. Listen to the silence, or notice the variety of sounds you hear. How many can you hear? What is their

quality? Are they soft or loud? Textured, fluctuating, or stable? Listen openly without trying to interpret what you hear.

- **Body.** Now become aware of your body. Notice your posture, the curve of your spine, the temperature of your body parts. Scan your body slowly, starting with your feet and progressing up to your head. Notice areas of tension, looseness, or tingling.
- **Breath.** Become aware of the sensations in your body as you inhale and exhale. Notice your pauses between breaths, as well as the temperature of the air you breathe in, and how your inhale is slightly cooler than your exhale.
- **Emotions.** Shift your focus to your mood and notice what you're feeling. If you don't identify any emotions, then notice that. Don't judge the emotions as good or bad; simply observe without trying to change the experience.
- **Thoughts.** Guide your attention toward your mind. Thoughts are sometimes seen as interfering with meditation, but on the contrary, they can become the object of the meditation. Notice when any thoughts arise, take a step back, and observe without letting your thoughts sweep you away. Simply let your thoughts be, without fueling them by constructing stories about your experiences.

After completing this exercise, set an intention for how you want to integrate mindfulness into your daily life. A good point of reference is to aim for at least 10 minutes of mindfulness practice per day.

Lucidity in Waking Reality

As you delve more into lucid dreaming, you may notice that the images of your dreams tend to mirror elements of your waking life, and vice versa. Consequently, the notion of lucidity in dreams can be applied to make your thinking and relating with waking reality more creative and adaptive.

The concept of "waking lucidity" implies a higher degree of clarity, insight, and psychological flexibility. For many lucid dreamers, applying their learning from lucid dreams to the waking world unfolds naturally as their practice matures. Here are some ideas to get you started.

PARALLELS

Identify elements from your dreams that reflect real-life issues to develop a deeper, more meaningful dialogue between states. Let's say you have a stressful dream in which you are trying to avoid your boss. Consider how aspects of your life may parallel the dream's emotions or dynamics. Is the dream directly related to your situation at work? Could your boss symbolize a part of yourself that needs to take authority? Perhaps you feel overly controlled in some situation and want to get out of it. Play with multiple perspectives to help you see the parallels between your dreams and waking life. Being aware of these parallels can help you apply aspects of lucidity to improve your waking conditions. For instance, how might you rescript your dream of your boss if you were lucid? And how might your response help you consider better ways to relate to the situation that it truly reflects?

"IF THIS WERE A DREAM, I WOULD . . ."

A lucid dreaming practice commits you to setting intentions for how you will apply the state of lucidity in useful ways. You can apply this to your waking life by reflecting on what you would do in "awake" situations if you were actually dreaming. Ask yourself, when facing a given problem or situation, "If this were a dream, what would I do differently?" Ask this while still acknowledging the physical and social limitations of objective reality. But within that container, consider how this question can help you approach the situation with more mental flexibility.

SET AND CARRY OUT INTENTIONS

When we're awake, we accomplish goals and set our minds to do future things all the time. However, many people still struggle with focus, productivity, and remembering to organize their behavior efficiently. Lucid dreaming can help you learn how to clarify and remember your intentions not just in your dreams, but also in everyday life, allowing you to live more in alignment with your higher values.

TAKE MORE RESPONSIBILITY

When you understand in lucid dreams that your reality is being constructed not from external sources, but from your own mental models of the world, it makes it easier to take responsibility for your experiences through the choices that you make. Applying this frame on reality while awake can be quite self-empowering—as long as you do it without blaming yourself for things that are outside your control. In other words, it's important to remember that there are always external forces shaping your reality. But by cultivating waking lucidity, you can consider how to take more responsibility for what you can change in your life.

PRACTICE POINT: APPLY THE THREE Rs TO A WAKING SITUATION

You can strengthen your intentions to apply waking lucidity to your daily life by applying the three Rs. First, call to mind a recent waking experience that did not go the way you would have liked. It should be an experience that happened only once. However, this single event may also be one that represents a recurring, problematic pattern in your life. Next, apply the three Rs to the experience.

Rescript. Choose a waking experience in which you will consider what you would have done differently had you been dreaming. Ask yourself: "What are some alternative responses that would have made the situation go better?" Then rescript the rest of the experience so that its outcome is more favorable, but still realistic.

Rehearse. Fully imagine the rescripted version of your experience. You can do this for a brief moment, or if you want, put yourself in a relaxed state and spend a few minutes thoroughly visualizing it.

Remind. Remind yourself that the next time you experience a similar situation while awake, you'll notice and remember to respond with a heightened level of waking lucidity. For example, you might remind yourself that the next time your partner gets frustrated, you'll remember to soften your tone. Or, the next time you feel disliked and have the urge to withdraw, you'll consider how you would relate differently if you knew it was a dream.

ADVENTURES IN LUCIDITY

When I encounter struggles in my day-to-day life, I ask myself, "What would I do if this were a dream?" I think about alternative solutions, like not letting what people say bother me, or asking for help with something even when I don't want to. I have found this way of thinking helpful in getting myself to do things that I normally wouldn't do.

After starting to do this, I had a nonlucid dream in which I was trying to practice waking lucidity. I was at a party when an acquaintance whom I greatly admire arrived, but he was busy talking to other people. I felt ignored and unimportant, but then I remembered to consider how I would deal with this situation if I were lucid dreaming. I realized that I would just go interrupt with a big smile and say hi. It hit me that there was no reason I couldn't do that. I marched up to him and he lit up when he saw me, giving me a warm hug. I felt so happy and relieved that I could change my reality just by changing how I think.

When I woke up, I felt surprised that my practice of waking lucidity wasn't just helping me in my waking life but was also changing how I think and act in my nonlucid dreams—it was changing me on a deeper level. The practice seemed more powerful than I had originally anticipated, and I planned to keep exploring it.

Letting Go of Fears

To commit to your practice of lucid dreaming, it will help to overcome any fears or misgivings that you may have about it. If you find that you have hesitancies about lucid dreaming, remember that our dreams have had our species' best interests at heart for hundreds of thousands of years. The concerns that people tend to have about lucid dreaming are often misguided, and if stumbling blocks do come up, it's always possible to modify your practice to minimize troubles. The following sections should clarify common misconceptions and alleviate any worries or ambivalence that you may have about lucid dreaming.

IS LUCID DREAMING SAFE?

Lucid dreaming is a perfectly natural and safe state of consciousness. Sometimes people are worried that practicing lucid dreaming could make them lose their ability to distinguish between waking and dreaming while they're awake. Here's why that concern is misguided: The central feature of lucid dreaming is learning to accurately determine which reality you're in, and to differentiate what's real from unreal. Moreover, your ability to know that you're awake is hardwired into your evolutionary makeup. Humans would not have survived without the ability to accurately comprehend the realness of threats in external physical reality.

Like all powerful activities that are oriented toward personal, existential, or spiritual growth, lucid dreaming can loosen your fixed ideas about reality. This happens so that you can construct more helpful models of viewing the world in their place. For some people, there's a negligible risk that a focus on lucid dreaming could contribute to feeling out of touch with reality—this outcome is extremely rare, but if you happen to notice reality confusion during waking hours, you can speak to a mental health specialist to help you decide whether you should back off from your lucid dreaming practices, or determine if your experience was in the normal range of reality confusion (for example, you occasionally believe a dream event really happened until you reflect later and realize it was just a dream).

IS LUCID DREAMING ADDICTIVE?

Some people worry that the world of lucid dreaming will be so enticing that it will become preferable to waking life, which could lead to addiction. Let's be clear: Lucid dreaming is not addictive. Lucid dreams make up only a minor portion of most people's dreams, so there is little to which you can become hooked on even if lucid dreams were addictive in the first place. Moreover, frequent lucid dreamers report that their lucid dreams connect them more fully to waking life, rather than disconnecting them from it.

It's true that people do make excessive use of alternative realities to cope with or escape from the waking world—just look at video games, cell phones, drugs, or too much food, sex, or sleep. The concern that you're engaging in a form of escapism would not lie with lucid dreaming itself, but rather with how you're coping with day-to-day stress or making use of alternative realities to avoid less preferable experiences.

An obsessive fixation with lucid dreaming that interferes with functioning in life would be an anomaly, but if you happen to find yourself ignoring important activities for the sake of lucid dreaming, it may be best to discontinue the practice or talk to a professional to help you figure out what's making you fixate on lucid dreaming in the first place.

WILL I FEEL PAIN IN LUCID DREAMS?

There's a common but erroneous belief that it's not possible to feel pain in dreams. We tend to dream the same types of sensations that we feel when we're awake, which include pain. Experiencing pain in dreams is uncommon—or at least underreported—and one of LaBerge's experiments revealed that pinching yourself in a dream is less painful than pinching yourself in waking life. While it is possible to feel pain in dreams, it seems that in the dream world, we are more primed to feel pleasure than pain.

WILL LUCID DREAMING MAKE ME TIRED?

Some people who consider attempting lucid dreaming wonder whether their quality of sleep will be compromised while they're lucid, and whether they will therefore be more tired the following day. They can rest assured that they won't.

Lucid dreams are just as restorative as normal dreams. They have not been associated with next-day fatigue, and in fact, people often report feeling excited and energized when they wake from lucid dreams, a feeling that can last through the following day.

Many factors contribute to fatigue, including diet, stress, exercise, psychological or medical conditions, and of course, insufficient or low-quality sleep. On occasion, some people, usually beginners, do report that they feel fatigued from excessively applying lucid dreaming induction methods night after night. However, feeling tired in this case would not be caused by the lucid dreaming itself, but rather by not getting enough sleep. If your induction practices are negatively impacting how much rest you are getting, reserve them for nights when you know you can get extra sleep in the morning, and take breaks rather than practicing every night.

Common Mistakes

A strong and stable lucid dreaming practice does not develop overnight. Making mistakes is a normal part of any learning process, and also part of the fun involved in lucid dreaming. But there are things you can do to minimize how much mistakes will impede your progress.

MOVING TOO FAST

Sometimes beginners find themselves so excited about lucid dreaming that they speed through learning about induction techniques without taking the time to fully understand and master them. While it is possible for some people to skim through the instruction and still pick up on lucid dreaming rather quickly, this can make you prone to misunderstanding and applying the skills incorrectly. Take your time while learning each skill. When your confidence increases, add more to your plate until you have a strong, integrated repertoire of induction tools.

GETTING FRUSTRATED

It's normal to feel frustrated if you are trying to achieve something but it isn't working. In psychology, it's well-known that placing excessive pressure on yourself to achieve something actually impairs performance. If you are anxious to induce lucidity, or are too hard on yourself when you don't succeed, it could interfere with your ability to have lucid dreams. Be compassionate toward yourself and be realistic about where you are in your practice. Know that everyone learns differently. If you get frustrated, perhaps take a few nights off. Taking a break may help you have a more relaxed focus the next time you try to lucid dream.

LACKING MOTIVATION

You can have an exceptional understanding of what it takes to lucid dream, but if you're not motivated to practice, you're not likely to experience lucid dreams. Consider what it is about lucid dreaming that could pique your interest and ignite your passion. Finding ways to connect with other lucid dreamers may also be a way to gain inspiration and strengthen your commitment.

DISTRACTIONS

We live in a fast-paced, goal-oriented world and are constantly bombarded by stimuli. If you're like most people, observing your present reality without getting distracted by other thoughts and concerns is a challenge. When the mind is always "busy" or "on," we seldom stop to notice what is truly going on around us. If you don't practice being more observant of your present moment while you're awake, it'll be more difficult to notice when you're dreaming.

USING UNRELIABLE TECHNIQUES

The most efficient and effective way to lucid dream is by using the methods that have been tested in controlled experiments and are known to work. While no technique works all the time and no scientific experiment is perfect, certain induction methods have a stronger basis for being effective. To quicken your path to learning lucid dreaming, use techniques that are backed by solid evidence.

Spread Your Wings

The practices we've introduced so far only begin to skim the surface of lucid dreaming's potential. By now, you should be developing a stronger taste for lucidity and feel eager to take your practice further. While there are many directions you can explore to increase your skills, the strategies in this chapter are perhaps the most promising ways to trigger growth spurts in your practice.

For many, completing the nightly experience log is an effective way to increase awareness and recall of what is happening during the night, which is critical for lucid dreaming. And since developing a higher proficiency in lucid dreaming requires becoming more familiar with the contents of your mind, mindfulness meditation can be helpful. With increasing recall and awareness, the mysterious interface between your waking and dreaming worlds starts becoming clearer. Relatedly, expanding the concept of lucidity to waking situations will help you enhance your overall degree of clarity, focus, and creative flexibility.

The next chapter outlines a practice sequence that integrates many of the tools that we have covered so that you can quickly reference, and ultimately memorize, routines that will invite more lucidity into your life.

CHAPTER 6

PRACTICE
SEQUENCE

Now that you've read this far, let's take everything you've learned and review how to put it all into practice. The following sequence outlines what a 24-hour cycle of intensive skill practice in lucid dreaming might look like when fully implemented. This is a flexible instructional sequence that's intended to quickly remind you how to develop and maintain your daily routines. Note that previous chapters describe each of these skills in depth.

This outline includes three main periods for practice: daytime, bedtime, and nighttime. You don't need to implement each skill every day, but you will want to practice consistently to improve. With time, they will become a natural, effortless part of your life. While certain skills are more central to inducing lucidity than others, all the steps in this sequence will support your growth as a lucid dreamer.

The mainstays for becoming proficient at this sequence include repetition, integration, and reevaluation. Focus on learning one skill at a time, and practice repeatedly in varying contexts until you master it. As you improve, gradually integrate your new skills with your existing practices. In time, it will become clearer how all the tools weave together in ways that prepare your mind for lucid dreaming.

Evaluate your progress periodically to identify areas that need to improve. If you get stuck, review this book's skills and concepts, and determine what you need to target to overcome your roadblocks. At any rate, refining your practice will be an ongoing process of building trust in yourself to know what to do, when to do it, and how to do it.

Daytime

Apply the following practices as you go about your daily routines. You'll start with a morning routine that allows space for recalling dreams and strengthening your mind to recognize dreamsigns. You will intersperse memory exercises into moments throughout the day to reinforce your intention to lucid dream. It's also wise to set time aside for other activities that can nurture an active lucid dream life.

AT RISE TIME

Update your dream journal. Before you get out of bed, finish your dream journal entries for the night. Highlight your dreamsigns.

Complete a cycle of MILD. Using the last dream you remember, apply the three Rs: Rescript and rehearse the dream as if it were lucid, then remind yourself to become lucid the next time you are dreaming.

THROUGHOUT THE DAY

Rereading state test. When performed correctly, this procedure (see page 57) integrates key intention-setting skills for inducing lucid dreams. Do the rereading state test at least five times per day, whenever you notice "waking dreamsigns," or whenever you think about lucid dreaming.

- **Am I dreaming?** Consider whether dreamsigns are present. Does anything indicate that you are dreaming?
- **Reread text.** If you believe you are awake, read some printed text, look away, then read it again. Repeat these steps, except this time, imagine the text will be different

when you reread it. If it stays the same, you can confirm you are awake.

- **Apply the three Rs.** Rescript your waking experience as if it were a lucid dream and rehearse this in your mind for a brief moment. Remind yourself to remember you are dreaming in your dreams tonight.

Be mindful. Be more in touch with what's happening in the present moment, rather than thinking of the past or future, analyzing situations, or wishing things were different. By learning to observe reality as it is, you'll develop a sharper eye for recognizing your true state of consciousness.

- **Quiet "busy brain."** Constant distraction can interfere with your lucid dreaming practice. Use mindfulness techniques during idle points of your day. Pay attention to your senses and inner experiences as they are. Do not cling to experiences or push them away. Just be present without judging your experiences as good or bad, and without striving to achieve anything.
- **Do one thing at a time.** Instead of multitasking, choose to focus only on what you're doing. For example, when you eat lunch, only pay attention to eating lunch. If you take a walk, only focus on the sensations of walking and your present environment.
- **Balance observing and participating.** While you go about your daily activities, be focused on the here and now; be totally in the moment as you do just what needs to be done.
- **Pause before reacting.** In nonlucid dreams, you tend to automatically react and buy into the stories of your dreaming mind. This can parallel how you react during your waking life. To be more mindful, notice your

thoughts and your urges to react. Increase your clarity of what's truly happening in the moment and consider how to respond in a way that aligns with your values.

SET TIME ASIDE

If you don't make it a point to set time aside to nurture your lucid dream life, it'll be harder to make consistent improvements. Here are a few things to work into your schedule.

Rescript your dreams. Rescript your recent dreams to be lucid and have a better outcome, for example, by incorporating responses that reflect self-integration or accomplishing a goal.

Ponder the meaning of your dreams. Sometimes the meanings of your dreams won't be clear immediately after you remember or record them. Take the time to really think about what your dreams could be reflecting about you or your life. This can enhance the insight and guidance you receive from dreams, keeping you motivated to regularly apply your lucidity and recall skills.

Meditate. To increase familiarity with your mind's contents and supplement your lucid dream practice, incorporate mindfulness and meditation into your daily life. Aim to meditate at least 10 minutes per day.

Bedtime

There are things you can do at bedtime to prime yourself for lucid dreaming. Below is a brief list, which includes tips about how to strengthen your intention to lucid dream, how to improve your ability to remember your dreams, and how to get good-quality sleep.

Wind down. Power down electronics 30 to 60 minutes before bedtime and engage in a calm, quiet activity.

Prepare your materials. Place your dream journal, pen, clock, light source, and any other practice aids within convenient reach of your bed.

Choose an induction strategy for the night. Will you aim to recall multiple dreams, or just focus on your last REM period in the morning? Is tonight well-suited for sleep interruption or for trying to induce a WILD? Have a plan in mind, but know that it's okay to play it by ear and see what feels right in the moment.

Remind yourself of your lucid dreaming goal. What do you plan to do if you lucid dream tonight? Give yourself a reason to become lucid.

Practice MILD. Intend to recognize that you're dreaming during tonight's dreams, and to carry out a pre-set goal. Have an action plan clearly in mind. Remind yourself that you'll have REM periods every 90 minutes, and several opportunities to recognize dreamsigns. Intend to wake up from your dreams, write them down, and apply the three Rs of MILD (see page 50). Before falling asleep, apply the three Rs to a recent dream. Then fall asleep while keeping your intention to lucid dream in mind.

Relax. Apply a technique to relax your mind and body, such as progressively scanning parts of your body with attention. Don't think about the day that just passed, or what you have to do tomorrow. Allow yourself to let go and look forward to the chance to be lucid during your upcoming dreams.

Nighttime

Nighttime, of course, is when your lucid dreams will play out. Below, we review the set of induction skills that you could apply, including MILD, dream journaling, WILD techniques, and sleep interruption.

DURING AWAKENINGS

Notice that you are awake. You have several brief awakenings over the night. Instead of immediately going back to sleep, set your mind to explicitly notice that it is a good time to apply recall and induction practices.

Write in your dream journal. Awakenings are ideal times to write down your dreams—you shouldn't wait to record them, because you'll forget the details. Occasionally, you may want to minimize the demands of journaling in the middle of the night. In that case, opt to write down only key dreamsigns or to memorize the dream for use with the MILD technique before returning to sleep.

Complete a nightly experience log (see page 104). Write down the time, code your experience type, and rate your degree of recall in an event row.

Practice MILD. Apply the three Rs: Rescript and rehearse the dream that you just woke up from as though it was lucid; use a previous dream if you don't remember your most recent one. Remind yourself that you will become lucid when you return to sleep.

Sleep interruption. After your third REM period (about four and a half hours after bedtime), get out of bed for 30 to 60 minutes and do a quiet, wakeful activity, like reading about lucid dreaming or dream journaling. Then go back to bed to practice MILD.

Use WILD techniques. Try to induce WILD (see page 66) as you fall back asleep, especially if you just woke from an early-morning dream, or after a planned period of sleep interruption.

Relax. Use your relaxation skills to quickly fall back asleep when desired.

Use alarms as needed. If you're finding it difficult to remember your dreams, set an alarm to wake you when you're likely to be dreaming.

Figure 6.1: Diagram of Nighttime Induction Protocol

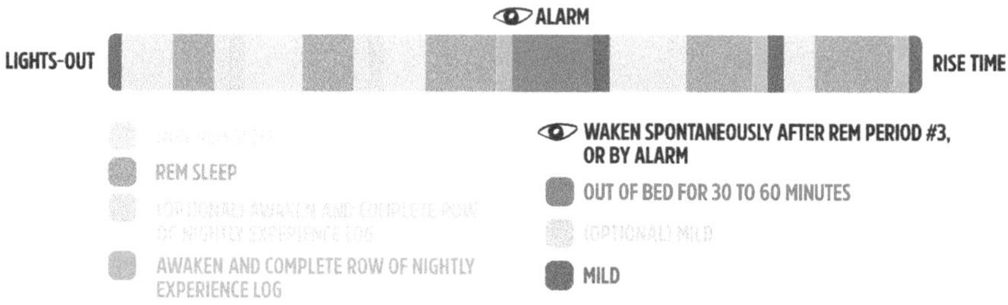

This diagram represents a night of using MILD techniques in conjunction with sleep interruption and completing a nightly experience log. Note that this figure is not to scale, and that the timing and number of REM periods are approximate.

DURING LUCID DREAMS

Here's a quick review of the critical skills that are necessary for using your time in lucid dreams effectively.

Remember your pre-set goal. The first thing to do after you become lucid is to carry out your preselected task. Be willing, however, to flexibly respond to your dreams' spontaneous imagery.

Repeat: "I am dreaming." To avoid drifting back into a non-lucid state, constantly remind yourself that you are dreaming.

Postpone waking up. At the first sign of fading visual imagery, spin your dream body or rub your dream hands. Focus on your sensations and don't think about waking up. If you do wake up, confirm that you're not experiencing a false awakening.

Critical Dos and Don'ts

Learning lucid dreaming can be vastly rewarding, but like anything worth practicing, comes with its share of challenges. Your overall journey will be smoother if you abide by the following guidelines.

DO:

- **Honor your individual pace for learning.** Everyone has different backgrounds, learning styles, and lifestyle factors that will either interfere with or promote lucid dreaming. Be patient with yourself—and hopeful.
- **Balance structure with flexibility.** Stick to the skills that are known to work, but trust your intuition to modify techniques, or the practice sequence, to work better for you.
- **Take breaks.** Sometimes your mind will be too worn out to focus on lucid dreaming. It can help to take a night, or several nights, off.
- **Regularly revisit your lucid dreaming goals.** Having a clear goal of what you will do once lucid will help you be more motivated to try and induce a lucid dream.

DON'T:

- **Try to master everything at once.** Split learning skills into smaller, more manageable chunks.
- **Try too hard.** Putting excess pressure on yourself to lucid dream can impair your performance.
- **Do a rereading state test** (see page 57) until after you've examined the environment for dreamsigns. You will lucid dream better if you improve your ability to recognize dreamsigns that are already present, not by relying on state tests.
- **Let your induction practices interfere with getting enough rest.** Although it's not critical if you sacrifice a little sleep once in a while, remember that humans function best when they're regularly getting between seven and nine hours of shut-eye per night.
- **Feel bad if you haven't had a lucid dream yet.** In fact, you may have had many lucid dreams but just don't remember them. Stay positive and enjoy the journey.

Continuing the Journey

Think of the practice sequence outlined earlier in this chapter as a map that shows you the main roads but still allows you to roam off the beaten path, so that you can figure out what works best for you. Remember that by staying committed, you'll eventually be able to hit cruise control on these techniques. Your practice will require less effort, and lucid dreaming can become a regular and rewarding part of your life.

Just as the map isn't the actual territory, there is more to applying these skills than we have space to cover here. After mastering the basic skills, you may find that you want to develop more sophistication in your practice. When you're ready, it can help to seek out a relationship with a skilled teacher—this can be instrumental.

Periodically, it can help to work toward mastering lucid dreaming skills while on retreat, or when you can otherwise take time away from your daily concerns to focus on your inner development. This isn't practical for everyone, so the next best option to upgrade your skill set is to get involved in local workshops or online programs, which are becoming more widely available. Connecting with other lucid dreamers is a terrific way to inspire lucidity, help you remember your dreams, and figure out how to benefit from them.

The End of the Beginning

The art of lucid dreaming can wake you up to new possibilities and pathways. At first, exploring lucid dreaming may feel foreign or alien. But with increasing recall and lucidity, you will start encountering a deep sense of familiarity, as though you're remembering a bigger, more beautiful part of yourself that you have always known but perhaps you had forgotten about.

The good news is that reaching lucidity in dreams can be easy and intuitive—it's achievable just by realizing that it's possible, and by setting your mind to it. In these pages, we broke down the skills for inducing and exploring lucidity into their elemental parts. But the hope is that as you develop your practice, you will find yourself peering through a looking glass that is much greater than the sum of its parts.

It can't be emphasized enough that the lucid dream state can open you up to new worlds that you didn't know existed. These worlds can be a potent catalyst for transformation, sharpening your acuity for discerning the real from the unreal, helping you break free from distorted models of yourself, and encouraging you to grow ever more perceptive of how the threads from your dreams and waking experiences are woven from the same fabric.

When you discover its essence, lucid dreaming can unearth a sense of raw and infinite self-empowerment. If you dive into its world, you'll feel a force drawing you ever closer to wholeness, and to your most authentic self. There's so much more. But this book is merely a beginner's guide, and we are at the end. The most wonderful thing now is that this is just the beginning for you.

ADDITIONAL RESOURCES

Lucid Dreaming

Lucidity.com | The Lucidity Institute

MindfulLucidDreaming.com | Kristen LaMarca, PhD

Exploring the World of Lucid Dreaming by Stephen LaBerge and Howard Rheingold

Mindfulness

Mindfulness Coach | Self-guided training app for iOS and Android, https://mobile.va.gov/app/mindfulness-coach

Mindful.org | Guidance on mindfulness meditation practices

Wherever You Go, There You Are: Mindfulness Meditation in Everyday Life by Jon Kabat-Zinn

Tibetan Buddhist Dream Yoga

Ligmincha.org | The Ligmincha International Foundation, Tenzin Wangyal Rinpoche's organization to preserve the teachings of Tibetan Buddhism

The Tibetan Yogas of Dream and Sleep by Tenzin Wangyal Rinpoche

Dream Yoga: Illuminating Your Life Through Lucid Dreaming and the Tibetan Yogas of Sleep by Andrew Holecek

REFERENCES

Aspy, Denholm J., Paul Delfabbro, Michael Proeve, and Phillip Mohr. 2017. "Reality Testing and the Mnemonic Induction of Lucid Dreams: Findings from the National Australian Lucid Dream Induction Study." *Dreaming* 27 (3): 206–231.

Becchetti, Andrea, and Alida Amadeo. 2016. "Why We Forget Our Dreams: Acetylcholine and Norepinephrine in Wakefulness and REM sleep." *Behavioral and Brain Sciences* 39 (e202). doi.org/10.1017/S0140525X15001739.

Blagrove, Mark, and E. F. Pace-Schott. 2010. "Trait and Neurobiological Correlates of Individual Differences in Dream Recall and Dream Content." *International Review of Neurobiology*, 92: 155–180. doi:10.1016/S0074-7742(10)92008-4.

Bulkeley, Kelly. 1997. *An Introduction to the Psychology of Dreaming*. Westport, Connecticut: Praeger Publishers.

Eichenlaub, Jean-Baptiste, Alain Nicolas, Jérôme Daltrozzo, Jérôme Redouté, Nicolas Costes, and Perrine Ruby. 2014. "Resting Brain Activity Varies with Dream Recall Frequency between Subjects." *Neuropsychopharmacology* 39: 1594–1602. doi:10.1038/npp.2014.6.

Evans-Wentz, W. Y. 2000. *Tibetan Yoga and Secret Doctrines: Seven Books of Wisdom of the Great Path*. New York: Oxford University Press.

Giguère, Brenda, and Stephen LaBerge. 1995. "To Touch a Dream: An Experiment in Touch, Pain, and Pleasure." *NightLight* 7 (1).

Hobson, J. Allan. 2003. *Dreaming: An Introduction to the Science of Sleep*. New York: Oxford University Press.

LaBerge, Stephen. 1985. *Lucid Dreaming*. New York: Ballantine Books.

LaBerge, Stephen. 1988. "Lucid Dreaming in Western Literature." In *Conscious Mind, Sleeping Brain*, edited by Jayne Gackenbach and Stephen LaBerge, 11–26. New York: Plenum Press.

LaBerge, Stephen. 2014. "Lucid Dreaming: Paradoxes of Dreaming Consciousness." In *Varieties of Anomalous Experience: Examining the Scientific Evidence*, edited by S. J. Lynn, E. Cardeña, and S. Krippner, 145–173. Washington, DC: American Psychological Association.

LaBerge, Stephen. 2015. "Metaconsciousness During Paradoxical Sleep." In *Dream Research: Contributions to Clinical Practice*, edited by Milton Kramer and Myron Glucksman. New York: Taylor & Francis.

LaBerge, Stephen. 2003. "Tibetan Dream Yoga and Lucid Dreaming: A Psychophysiological Perspective." In *Buddhism and Science,* edited by B. A. Wallace. New York: Columbia University Press.

LaBerge, Stephen, Benjamin Baird, and Philip G. Zimbardo. 2018. "Smooth Tracking of Visual Targets Distinguishes Lucid REM Sleep Dreaming and Waking Perception from Imagination." *Nature Communications* 9 (1). doi:10.1038/s41467-018-05547-0.

LaBerge, Stephen, and Howard Rheingold. 1990. *Exploring the World of Lucid Dreaming.* New York: Ballantine Books.

LaBerge, Stephen, and Kristen LaMarca. 2015–2018. Nightly Experience Type Recall and Time (NETRAT) Log. Unpublished.

LaBerge, Stephen, Kristen LaMarca, and Benjamin Baird. 2018. "Pre-sleep Treatment with Galantamine Stimulates Lucid Dreaming: A Double-Blind, Placebo-Controlled, Crossover Study." *PLoS One* 13 (8):e0201246. doi:10.1371/journal .pone.0201246.

LaBerge, Stephen, Rachel Steiner, and Brenda Giguère. 1996. "To Sleep, Perchance to Read." *NightLight* 8 (1 & 2).

LaBerge, Stephen, and Lynne Levitan. 1995. "Validity Established of Dreamlight Cues for Eliciting Lucid Dreaming." *Dreaming* 5 (3): 159–168.

Laughlin, Charles D. 2011. *Communing with the Gods: Consciousness, Culture, and the Dreaming Brain*. Brisbane, Australia: Daily Grail Publishing.

Levitan, Lynne. 1992. "A Thousand and One Nights of Exploring Lucid Dreaming." *NightLight* 4 (2).

Levitan, Lynne, Stephen LaBerge, D. J. DeGracia, and Philip G. Zimbardo. 1999. "Out-of-Body Experiences, Dreams, and REM Sleep." *Sleep and Hypnosis* 1 (3): 186–196.

Sparrow, Scott. 1976. *Lucid Dreaming: Dawning of the Clear Light*. Virginia Beach, VA: A.R.E. Press.

Tholey, Paul. 1988. "A Model for Lucidity Training as a Means of Self-Healing and Psychological Growth." In *Conscious Mind, Sleeping Brain*, edited by Jayne Gackenbach and Stephen LaBerge, 263–287. New York: Plenum Press.

Tholey, Paul. 1983. "Techniques for Inducing and Manipulating Lucid Dreams." *Perceptual and Motor Skills* 57 (1): 79–90. doi:10.2466/pms.1983.57.1.79.

Vallat, Raphael, Tarek Lajnef, Jean-Baptiste Eichenlaub, Christian Berthomier, Karim Jerbi, Dominique Morlet, and Perrine M. Ruby. 2017. "Increased Evoked Potentials to Arousing Auditory Stimuli during Sleep: Implication for the Understanding of Dream Recall." *Frontiers in Human Neuroscience* 11 (132). doi:10.3389/fnhum.2017.00132.

Varela, Francisco J., ed. and Jerome Engel. 1997. *Sleeping, Dreaming, and Dying: An Exploration of Consciousness with The Dalai Lama,* foreword by H. H. the Fourteenth Dalai Lama; narrated and edited by Francisco J. Varela; with contributions by Jerome Engel, Jr. ... [et al.]; translations by B. Alan Wallace and Thupten Jinpa. Boston: Wisdom Publications.

Wangyal Rinpoche, Tenzin. 1998. *The Tibetan Yogas of Dream and Sleep*. Ithaca, New York: Snow Lion Publications.

INDEX

ABOUT THE AUTHOR

 KRISTEN LaMARCA, PhD, is a clinical psychologist with expertise in applied psychophysiology, sleep disorders, and lucid dreaming. She has co-facilitated Lucidity Institute's intensive programs on lucid dreaming since 2010, and she has published research on inducing lucid dreams through skills-training and the use of galantamine, a memory-enhancing substance. She currently practices clinically in southern California where she specializes in Lucid Dreaming Therapy for nightmares and stress-related conditions. She also runs a six-week online workshop in lucid dreaming that integrates induction science, mindfulness meditation, and personally-tailored coaching.

CPSIA information can be obtained
at www.ICGtesting.com
Printed in the USA
BVHW061440170919
558571BV00002B/2/P

9 781641 523820